THE **7** EASY ST

MORTGAGE FREEDOM

My thanks on the congratulations. I may have however had trouble getting past the goal post if it were not for your dedication and professionalism so all my thanks go out to you. You were absolutely correct about locking the rate. I consider myself lucky to have you as my Mortgage Broker and to have listened to your advice. You have no need to worry — after having nothing but hugely positive results with your services you can rest assured I will sing your praises to anyone who will listen. Hopefully in two or three years I will be contacting you again for the purchase of another property if all goes well.

Paul
N.T., Australia

As an extremely busy person, I simply do not have the time to digest and assess the numerous options for home and investment loans from every bank. Mortgage Australia helped me navigate this maze in an easy-to-follow fashion. And they keep us informed of new opportunities. I have absolutely no hesitation in recommending their services to anyone contemplating a home or investment loan.

Professor Peter B
Lismore, NSW

THE 7 EASY STEPS TO
MORTGAGE
FREEDOM

*Revealed by a mortgage industry
insider who did it in just 7 years*

Mortgage Australia
MORTGAGE AUSTRALIA GROUP

DAVID HAM

First published 2015 by Mortgage Australia Group Pty Ltd
37 Craven Street, Bedford WA 6052, Australia

National Library of Australia Cataloguing-in-Publication entry:

Creator: Ham, David, author.

Title: The 7 easy steps to mortgage freedom : revealed by a mortgage
                   industry insider who did it in just 7 years
                   / David Ham.

ISBN: 9780994334107 (paperback)

Subjects: Mortgage loans--Australia.
                   Housing--Australia--Finance.
                   Prepayment of debts--Australia.
                   Finance, Personal--Australia.

Dewey Number: 332.7220994

Printed in Australia.

10 9 8 7 6 5 4 3 2 1

Disclaimer

The material in this publication is of the nature of general comment only, and does not represent professional or financial advice. It is not intended to provide specific guidance for particular circumstances and it should not be relied on as the basis for any decision to take action or not take action on any matter which it covers. Readers should obtain professional advice where appropriate, before making any such decision. To the maximum extent permitted by law, the author and publisher disclaim all responsibility and liability to any person, arising directly or indirectly from any person taking or not taking action based upon the information in this publication. Names used in examples and case studies have been changed for privacy reasons.

Who else wants to be mortgage free?

My team at Mortgage Australia specialises in implementing the 7 Easy Steps to Mortgage Freedom for our clients to make it faster and easier for you.

Here is how we help you become mortgage free, easier and faster:

1. **We charge no fee to you** for finding and organising the right, low cost loan for you from over 1,350 finance options with a focus on helping you become mortgage free.

2. **We will make sure your loan has the necessary features and is set up correctly** to be as easy as possible to pay off faster using the smart money management methods I explain in this book (and avoid costly mortgage mistakes).

3. **We will futureproof your loan** by regularly reviewing it against the latest special offers and better discounts as they become available to you. You can make an informed decision about whether to switch, knowing all the costs and benefits of doing so.

4. As you build equity, if you decide you want to invest in property, **we can properly structure your lending and can provide as much assistance as you require** with selecting and organising properties, making it as simple as possible.

If you would like to start this process, the best way to get started is just to email me directly. Let me know about your current situation and we can work out the best place to start that suits you.

Email me anytime at <u>davidham@mortgageaustralia.com.au</u> for a no obligation discussion about helping you become mortgage free, faster and easier. Just like I did!

Enjoy the book and I hope to speak with you soon.

David Ham

Interest never sleeps nor sickens nor dies;
it never goes to the hospital;
it works on Sundays and holidays;
it never takes a vacation;
it never visits nor travels;
it has no love, no sympathy;
it is as hard and soulless as a granite cliff.

Once in debt, interest is your companion;
every minute of the day and night;
you cannot shun it or slip away from it;
you cannot dismiss it;
it yields neither to entreaties, demands nor orders;
and whenever you get in its way,
or cross its course or fail to meet its demands,
it crushes you.

J. Reuben Clark

CONTENTS

STEP 1
Why you must become mortgage free faster 27

CHAPTER 1
Why most people will end up broke 29

CHAPTER 2
Why you should really care about your home loan 33

STEP 2
Get the cheapest loan you can 39

CHAPTER 3
Choosing the right loan for you. 41

CHAPTER 4
Don't shy away from smaller lenders. .51

CHAPTER 20

CHAPTER 21

CHAPTER 22

RESOURCES

About the author

David Ham founded the Mortgage Australia Group in 2000 to help home owners find the lowest cost home loan available and to teach them how to become mortgage free.

Since then his business and network of local Mortgage Australia Brokers has organised over $3 Billion in Home and Investment Loans and has over 6,500 current home loan accounts.

Most importantly David practices what he preaches. Over a 7 year period from 2000 to 2007, he went from having nothing to owning a $920,000 home – completely mortgage free, while only making the minimum repayments along the way.

David's mission is to show you how he did it, so you can too!

Acknowledgements

To my great team of Mortgage Brokers who have stuck with me over the years, and have taught me everything I know about home loans and achieving my financial goals.

To James Veigli, The MAGNETIC Professional, thank you for your help in bringing this book to life.

To YOU – our existing and new clients, for trusting us with your financial lives. The relationships we're forged and your financial success will always be our first priority. We are here to serve you.

My story

Let me tell you a little about myself and how I got started. You will quickly see that if I was able to do this, you certainly will be able to.

To take you back a fair way, my mother raised me and my two older sisters on her own. Being a single mother, it was very tough for her. While I was going to school, she worked as a cleaning lady to make ends meet for us while at the same time she attended university. It was a real financial struggle for her but she did her best for all of us, and I couldn't be more grateful or inspired by her.

And it certainly taught me that I wanted to avoid that horrible feeling that comes with the bill that arrives that you just don't know how you'll pay and wondering how my family would make ends meet. I also wanted to be able to look after my mother later in life so she didn't have to worry about these things anymore.

While I was at University, I completed work experience with the global accounting firm Ernst & Young. It was there that I learned about the developing field of Mortgage Broking, which looked like a great opportunity.

On a shoestring budget, three of the senior staff from Ernst & Young and I started a mortgage broking business. This meant borrowing money on my credit card to pay my way and support myself in the early days.

Fresh out of University, I didn't have any money or assets to my name; in fact, I owed money on my car loan and on my credit card, and I had tens of thousands of dollars in University 'HECS' fees and Austudy loan fees to repay.

Several months after starting the company, it seemed we didn't have a clear direction; it was a typical case of too many decision makers and not enough people actually doing the work. So I decided to buy out my original partners and continued to run my fledgling business as a one-man-band.

While being very stressful at the time, this turned out to be the best decision, as I was able to push ahead much faster with my own ideas.

As things began to move in the right direction, my wife and I bought our first home with the help of the First Home Owners Grant. A tiny, two-bedroom flat in Maylands, Western Australia, was all we could afford, but we loved it. It was over the next couple of years, living in that house and working on my own as a Mortgage Broker that I learned everything I have since applied to make myself and many of my clients mortgage free.

At this stage I have a confession to make. When I started my company, Mortgage Australia, in 2000, I had no financial background whatsoever. My degree from the University of Western Australia was an Honours Degree in Psychology, followed by a couple of years at Curtin University of Technology doing the Masters of Organisational Psychology course.

I don't come from a banking or financial sales background, and I'm not stuck in that way of thinking.

However, I now know my six years studying psychology at university is my greatest strength. I became an avid student of 'Behavioural Finance'. This is a relatively new field of psychology that looks at how people make financial decisions, how they manage their money in relation to investing, spending, and borrowing.

But, don't worry; this is no touchy-feely therapy session I'm about to give you. I've learned that, for people to get the best financial results, especially concerning their mortgage, things need to be set up in a way that makes it easy for them to pay it off fast—as opposed to it being set up in a way that makes it easy for their bank to make the most interest.

The key word here is 'easy'. All people, myself included, want to take the easy road; the path of least resistance. It is very difficult for people to keep making sacrifices over a sustained period of time. It is much better to put a little extra effort in at the beginning to have it set up right, and then let it go largely on autopilot from there.

To me, paying off a home loan is like trying to lose weight. If you spend hours every day on a treadmill and eat only the right foods, you will lose weight. In the long run, though, very few people can stick to such a strict routine.

In the same way, you can pay every cent you earn into your home loan, work a second job and live like a pauper for years; but again, very few people can do that for the long haul. What you need instead is a realistic, sustainable, and natural process that is set up properly in the first place that requires minimal effort to maintain. Ideally, it is completely self-sustaining with just an occasionally required adjustment.

The fundamental financial lesson I have lived by is summed up in the Aesop fable, written in the 6th Century BC — 'The Ant and the Grasshopper'

One beautiful summer day, a lazy grasshopper was chirping and sitting and playing games, just as he did every day. A hard-working ant passed by, carrying a huge leaf that he was taking back to the ant's nest.

The grasshopper said to the ant,

"All you ants do is work all day.
You should be more like me and play, play, play!"

The ant replied,

"I'm storing food for the winter season.
You should be working, for just the same reason.
What will you eat when the weather gets cold?
How will you feed your hungry household?"

The grasshopper laughed,

"All you ants do is work and worry.
Slow down, don't be in such a hurry.
Just look around, there's plenty of food,
don't give me advice, that's just plain rude."

The ant kept working, the grasshopper kept playing, and winter soon came. The ant had prepared for the winter and had just enough food stored in the nest to last through the cold, harsh weather.

Now that winter had arrived, the grasshopper couldn't find any food, and soon became very hungry. But he soon remembered the hard-working ant he had made fun of during the summer. The grasshopper went to the ant's nest and asked for food.

The ant, who was still busy keeping the food clean and dry, said,

"I toiled to save food for the winter freeze,
while you spent the summer playing in ease.
I stored just enough food for the winter, it's true,
but I can't feed you all winter, or I'll starve too."

The ant gave the grasshopper a few crumbs, but the grasshopper was cold, miserable, and hungry all winter. The next summer, the grasshopper worked hard to store food for the upcoming winter. That next winter, grasshopper was well fed and happy!

He had learned to think ahead and plan for the future.

If you follow my plan, you don't need to work nearly as hard as the Ant, but the principle is to build for the future, so as soon as possible your money can start working for you, instead of you always working to get money (and hopefully, you can avoid some very expensive mortgage traps along the way).

Introduction

Everybody knows that the first step to financial freedom is paying off their mortgage. The sooner you do that, the sooner you can start building wealth and improving your lifestyle with all that money that was going to paying off your home.

Most people look forward to the day when they are no longer slaving away to pay their home off, but my experience of 15 years in the mortgage industry is that they don't have a clear plan on how to get there fast and without substantial additional effort and sacrifice. Don't worry though; at first, neither did I. But after buying my first home, I learned the right methods. And after having bought my first home just 7 years earlier, by the age of 33 I fully owned my $920,000 home. Plus, I also owned 8 investment properties and my family was financially secure.

The 7 easy steps to mortgage freedom that I give you in this book are the steps I took as someone who works with home loans every day. They are the fastest way I know to be mortgage free without taking unnecessary risks or compromising your lifestyle. You don't even need to apply every single step, but each step will add to the speed at which you can be mortgage free.

The picture on the next page is the front page of The West Australian newspaper's Real Estate section (October 28, 2007). That's me and my family in front of our house when we became mortgage free in December 2007.

Since then, having thousands of extra dollars every month, my family and I have been able to travel the world, to places like the Greek Islands,

Sunday Times
ReadersMART
OCTOBER 28, 2007
realestate.com.au
ReadersMART
13 11 13
Family affair
HOME SWEET HOME IN MAYLANDS 3

Spain, Italy, Germany, Austria, Switzerland, China, New Zealand, Chile, Vietnam, Thailand, Cambodia, Indonesia, Malaysia, the United States, and even to Antarctica and on safari in South Africa.

We didn't achieve any of this by making a lot of extra repayments and markedly compromising our lifestyle. I'm not saying there were no sacrifices, but this is not a story of scrimping and saving.

> We did it through a better understanding of how home loans work and of how we were managing our money – and then applying this knowledge. It was about making our money work for us instead of the other way around. This is not a story of taking risks.

In fact, because I had done things in a safe, methodical way, when the Global Financial Crisis (GFC) hit it didn't cause us any concerns whatsoever. I am not interested in gambling with my family's future. In fact, from working with many homeowners, I know that the way I do things is much less risky than how most people manage their money, and it definitely produces much better results.

I believe that what I did is very easy for most homeowners to replicate; you just need to know how to do it safely and easily. It is never too early or too late to start on a path to financial freedom. The only real criteria are that you own a home (or are planning to) and have an income. It might take more or less time, depending on how driven you are.

You may be selling your current home and about to buy a new one—that is an ideal time to begin this process, because you are going to be getting a new mortgage soon anyway, and one of the critical steps is having the right mortgage and having it set it up properly.

Tips for reading this book

This book is written in an easy-to-understand way. When reading, I hope you feel like I am having a personal conversation with you one-on-one.

Throughout the book you will see special call-out sections, designed to show you the most important take-away points as you go along. Here's how they work:

Key Point

This icon and style of call-out box represents the Key Point you need to know, so pay close attention to what you see in these boxes. This could be a big mistake to avoid, smart strategy to use, or important tip to help you.

Example

Boxes that look like this include Case Studies or Examples you can learn from. Often an idea or topic is best explained by working through and seeing how the numbers look. It's also a great way of showing you how a strategy or topic works in real life.

This icon and call-out is used to highlight important Quotes from the book, as well as sharing with you quotes and wisdom from other famous people.

Valuable Resource

When you see this icon and call-out, it's because I have a Valuable Resource to share with you. This could be a website to view; document, template or calculator to download; or contact information for you to get professional assistance. Not everything can fit inside this book – so keep an eye out for these extra resources to help.

Before we begin

So we are clear right from the start, this book is a general educational guide only and is definitely not a substitute for specific financial advice.

One purpose of providing the information in this book is to highlight one of the key differences between lenders at any given point in time. A key message here is to look as widely as possible when choosing which lender to borrow from if you are not happy with what your current bank is telling you.

We are absolutely not recommending or suggesting any particular lender in this book.

Any interest rates or fees shown are not current, nor the lowest rates or fees any lender may have had at the time this book was written. Each lender's maximum loans in the scenarios mentioned were based on their serviceability calculations at the time of writing and would still be subject to the lenders own terms and conditions. Their current maximum borrowing levels for each lender are now likely to be very different than the examples given here.

> If anyone ever gives you advice without first understanding your full situation and goals, my advice is simple: run!

Before taking any action on anything you learn in this book, or anywhere else for that matter, please seek professional advice from a licensed expert. That means getting your tax advice from an accountant, financial advice from a financial planner, credit and lending advice from a licensed finance broker, property advice from a real estate agent (or buyer's agent), and legal advice from a solicitor.

Accept no less than credible, authorized and specific expert advice at all times, and always make sure you are well informed before making any decisions.

Please retain this book in a convenient location so that you may refer to it in the future, and feel free to ask for additional copies as a means to introducing those you care about and feel will benefit from this information.

I hope you enjoy this book and learn important information to help you become mortgage free and live the life of your dreams.

Here's to your future!

David Ham
Founder *(and still mortgage free!)*
Mortgage Australia Group

STEP 1

Why you must become mortgage free faster

It's time to start thinking differently about money and debt and start the healing process - and the process toward wealth and freedom. 'Freedom from Bad Debt' can get you started.
Robert Kiyosaki, Author of Rich Dad Poor Dad

Everyone wants to be mortgage free, but now more than ever it is financially crucial that you do so as quickly as you can.

The first step to you becoming mortgage free is simply to get an idea of where most people go wrong so you can get it right.

CHAPTER 1

Why most people will end up broke

By 2035, anyone born after 1965 can only claim the Aged Pension after turning 70, not 65. As a result, unlike our parents and grandparents, most of us will get five less years of pension support in our lives.

It's clear that people need to be much more active in ensuring that they are prepared for their financial future. According to the Australian Bureau of Statistics, three times as many people retire on the pension compared to those who retire on their own funds. Not only that, half of all retired couples had an annual pension income of less than $28,260 a year, and half of all retired single people had an annual income of less than $21,700 per year.

I clearly remember working with some clients that were in this exact situation when I was starting out as a Mortgage Broker. The couple were in their 60's and were about to retire. They had a loan against their home that they had regularly drawn up on and nice new cars in the driveway with big loans against them. It was such a shame to see two hard working people end up with a very meagre retirement, simply because they had not managed their money well and had not prepared for their retirement. Sadly, the financial reality for this couple was that when they stopped working they would likely have to sell their home, go on the pension, and rent.

At the very least, it should be everyone's goal to pay off their home loan. If you own your home outright, you have so many more options, such as downsizing, moving to a retirement village, or taking out a reverse mortgage to realise an extra income in retirement.

However, the reality is that, in the future, 3 out of 4 people will end up with the pension as their main source of income.

A big reason for this is people's attitudes toward money. When I drive past my local petrol station and see cars lined up in long queues, I know that fuel prices are down, but I ask myself how much are they really saving for all that effort?

According to a recent study by the Australian Competition and Consumer Commission, if you buy petrol on the cheapest day of the week, compared to the most expensive, you can save up to $200 per year.

Key Point

I know from the thousands of home loans my company has organised that most Australians can easily save much more than $200 every single MONTH, by spending only 30 minutes of minimal effort every year or two, and from the comfort of their own home, rather than losing hours of their life sitting in line in their cars at a petrol station.

I'm not saying that it isn't important to put effort into saving money. It absolutely is. However, you should start by tightly organising your borrowing.

Using the methods I'll discuss in this book, knowing how to pay your home loan off quickly will allow you to start investing earlier - this is the key to financial freedom.

Another reason most people retire with little money is that they change their home many times in their lives, usually upgrading. This is quite normal, as your needs and family circumstances change. It would be nice if we could all afford our dream home right away, but that is very rarely the case.

Example: changing properties costs big money

On a median Australian home in a capital city, you are looking at paying $23,877 in government fees and taxes and a further $12,760 to a real-estate agent to sell your current home – a total of $36,637.

The problem comes when people sell their old home and buy the new one. They pay thousands of dollars in real estate agent fees and tens of thousands of dollars more in property stamp duty. This represents $30,000+ of easily ignored money - and because it is invariably added onto their new home loan, they then also pay tens-of-thousands of dollars of extra interest over the life of the loan. When you add this $36,637 to your new home loan, your repayments at a 6% interest rate will be an extra $219.90 per month for 30 years. And you will pay an extra $42,427 in interest – a total of $79,064.

Do this just a few times over your life and you are looking at hundreds-of-thousands of dollars in government and real-estate agent fees as well as extra home loan interest. All of this eats into the equity you build over time and affects your lifestyle in retirement.

A better approach when you need to upgrade is to keep your old property and rent it out, if at all possible.

That is exactly what I did and it has paid off many times over for me. I don't know anyone at retirement who wouldn't be hugely better off if they still owned at least one of their previous homes, even with their original mortgages still on them (which is now an investment loan).

Stamp duty and other government fees can't be avoided when you buy a home, but it is the fee you pay for owning the property, so you are getting a lot more for the fees you have paid if you own that property for 50 years than if you own it for 10. Better still, stay in your current home as long as you can and buy investment properties. Of course, this isn't always possible to do and it will certainly slow down the possibility of upgrading in the short term, but it will give you substantial wealth and financial options later in life.

Another reason many people struggle financially in retirement is that they wait too long to begin investing. Or more often, their only investment outside of paying off their own home is superannuation. Waiting longer, in my opinion, makes the process risky because you need to accumulate properties more quickly and you need more of them (and, therefore, greater debt) to achieve the same outcome you would have if you had started earlier.

Generally, people feel that it is safer to invest when their home loan is fully paid off. The problem with that is that they start their investment process much later, so there is much less time for them to see capital growth.

Investing shouldn't be stressful; it should make you feel less stress because you know you are building a foundation for your future. Roughly 8% of Australians own at least one investment property; however, less than 0.5% own three or more. I think this is mainly because people start too late. It is also because they choose the wrong sorts of older properties that have high out of pocket costs and are expensive to hold onto, which are not the kind I like investing in. And if you really don't want to end up broke and relying on the Aged Pension, the first thing to look at is the home loan you have right now.

CHAPTER 2

Why you should really care about your home loan

If you have a home or investment loan, it's probably your single biggest monthly expense. That's why this is perhaps the most important message you'll ever read, because, odds are, you're paying way too much.

When it comes to home loans, even small improvements can produce major benefits.

As a major financial decision (perhaps one of the most significant ones of your life), always having the lowest cost home loan for your situation is critical.

Get it right, and you can set yourself up for financial security and a comfortable lifestyle.

Get it wrong (as most people unfortunately do) and you could end up:

$ Paying a HUGE amount in extra interest to the Banks (for example, overpaying more than $201,103 in interest on a $450,000 loan over 30 years at 6%pa interest compared to the same loan at 5%).

$ Taking the full 30 years to pay off your loan (many people never fully pay off their home loan over their lifetime).

$ Being unable to properly invest for your future and becoming part of the 80% of Australians who end up on some form of government assistance in retirement (with access to retirement benefits being delayed to 70 years of age).

I know what you're thinking... *"Aren't all loans really the same?"*

Well actually... not at all!

Example: are loans all the same?

When I recently compared the true cost of 383 advertised variable home loans offered by 104 different lenders on a $450,000 home loan, the difference between the 10 least expensive loans and the 10 most expensive loans was a huge $599.50 every single month.

If you paid that $599.50 as extra repayments into the loan, you would save a massive $211,833 and cut over 10 years off your home loan.

These are the loans that lenders are paying to advertise; these are their best loans, discount packages, and special offers!

While you might be confident that your interest rate is not one of the more expensive ones, the difference between the cheapest loans and just the average loan was still a whopping $319.73 per month. This means that the average Australian home owner can pocket an extra $319.73 every month (or homeowners could use that money as extra repayments, saving $142,987 and being mortgage free 7 years earlier).

Key Point

In this book, you'll discover the little known secrets the banks want to keep from you. Secrets like:

· How a small reduction in your weekly mortgage interest can save you thousands over the life of your loan.

Key Point *(cont.)*

- The clever advertising tricks the banks use to hide the true cost of the loan (and make loans extremely difficult to compare).

- How banks make their high cost loans look cheap.

- How your home loan can get cheaper and cheaper the longer you have it.

- The most common and costly mistakes homeowners make with their loans.

Early in my Mortgage Broking career, I quickly saw that that most people paid much more than they needed to for their loans. Now, just in case you're still thinking, *"I'm sure I have a great home loan, so how much could I really save?"* think again. Reducing your interest cost by just $20 per week amounts to saving $49,736 of your hard-earned money over the life of your loan.

It is not your bank's job to show you how to save money on your home loan or how to make a smart choice.

Yes, when it comes to home loans, even tiny savings add up, and the bottom line is that banks are making a fortune.

Key Point

Australian banks are some of the most profitable in the world. In fact, here are the recent annual profits for the 'Big 4' banks:

- Commonwealth: $8.63 Billion

- NAB: $5.45 Billion

- ANZ: $6.30 Billion

- Westpac: $6.81 Billion

When you look at how the home loan market (one of the banks' biggest profit centres) really works, it's easy to see how these massive profits add up.

> ### Example: interest adds up!
>
> On a home loan of $450,000 over 30 years at 6%, you will repay a massive $971,734 back to the bank (calculated on the NAB's own loan calculator).
>
> This amount is made up of the original $450,000 "principal", plus an extra $521,734 in interest. You are paying back more than double the amount you borrowed.

Loan products are complex and they are difficult to easily compare, making them something the consumer really needs to research and shop around for.

Nevertheless, many Australians will spend more time shopping for the latest widescreen TV than they will for a loan.

Instead, how about spending some time getting your home loan right (or getting a professional to do it for you) and because you have saved so much money you can go and buy the TV you really want without feeling quite so guilty.

Hopefully you can see just how important a low cost home loan is. Take the time to get a low cost loan or find a trusted expert who will do it for you.

Valuable Resource: find some of the best deals

To find some of the cheapest loans available for you and see how much you can save, email me at:

davidham@mortgageaustralia.com.au

Just let me know your general financial situation and I'll investigate your options for you – free of charge and no obligation.

I personally read and reply to every email I receive – and I'd love to hear from you too.

At Mortgage Australia we compare over 1,350 finance options from dozens of major lenders. In fact, around 90% of all home loans in Australia are with lenders we work with.

STEP 2

Get the cheapest loan you can

The second step to becoming mortgage free is to get the right loan in the first place at the lowest cost.

Every dollar you spend in extra interest or fees is money that is a dollar that isn't paying off your loan.

CHAPTER 3
Choosing the right loan for you

There are many home loan choices out there, and it can all seem very overwhelming when you're about to purchase a property. It might be tempting to keep all of your banking in the same place for simplicity's sake. Many borrowers apply with their current bank just to get it over and done with.

However, don't just assume that your current bank branch has your best interests at heart, the more interest you pay the more profitable they are. Finding the best loan is not only about choosing a lender; in fact, the lender is the least important part.

It's most important to first decide what type of loan is right for you with the features you will benefit from, and then find that type of loan with the most competitive pricing.

The right choice of loan can make all the difference in the long term.

When buying a home most people will negotiate to get the best price they can. But the real price of your home is the cost of the home plus the interest you pay back to the bank. Or put another way, with a cheaper loan you can afford a more expensive home for the same real price.

For that reason I strongly suggest you take the time to shop around for your home loan before you start house hunting.

Example: the power of a cheaper rate

Do you know that you would pay back the exact same amount to buy a $500,000 home on a 6% home loan over 30 years, as buying a $558,000 home on a 5% home loan?

In both cases the repayments are $3,000 per month for 30 years but at the cheaper rate you get a better home which is also worth more in the future.

So how do you get the right loan?

Easy. Use a mortgage broker!

Yes, I know, I run a Mortgage Broking company so of course I think this. But I *chose* to work in the Mortgage Broking industry because I like to stack the odds in my (and your) favour. If my business has the advantage of providing a better offering to my customers, that is an advantage I want. Not that I ever worked for a bank, but in my opinion the lending staff of the banks have a really hard job, much harder than mine. As I said, I prefer to do things the easy way.

Later in this book I will discuss the methods we use for finding people the right loan at the cheapest cost, within the panel of lenders we have. You can certainly apply this method yourself, or use a reputable Mortgage Broker to do it for you.

When you go to a bank and you want a 3-year fixed rate loan, the bank has a 3-year fixed rate loan to offer you, but only one. So the bank will tell you that *their* 3-year fixed rate loan is the best one for you.

A Mortgage Broker on the other hand will have 20, 30, 40 or even more lenders they work with. So that means they have 20, 30, 40 or more 3-year fixed rate loans they can compare, and you just choose the cheapest and most appropriate one.

It's a lot easier to be a Mortgage Broker like me and have a wider range of options for people to choose from than work for the bank and have to try and convince your customer that the single choice you have is the right one for them.

Still, many people wonder why they should use a broker instead of just going to the bank they use already. The short answer is that a broker works for you, bank staff work for the bank. It's your Mortgage Broker's job to go to bat for you to get you the right mortgage. The bank staff do have one big advantage, and that is the millions of dollars they spend in advertising which builds familiarity and trust with the public.

Fortunately, people are becoming more and more familiar with how Mortgage Brokers work. Also, the introduction of the Australian Credit Licence and National Consumer Credit Protection Act in 2009, which is overseen by ASIC, has further ensured borrowers' rights are protected.

Whether you have ever used a Mortgage Broker or not, I would also argue that the Mortgage Broking industry has resulted in lower cost loans for everyone. In the past a new lender with a cheap loan had to contend with the prohibitive costs of large scale advertising and building their own network of mobile lending staff, which in turn impacts on the cost of their loans. Now a new lender simply needs to offer their loans through Mortgage Brokers and they have an immediate nationwide sales network at their disposal. And if that lender has a truly competitive loan, Mortgage Brokers will scramble to offer it to their clients because it will help them win your businesses. The end result is a far more competitive mortgage market, with greater choice and cheaper loans for everyone.

Valuable Resource: broker vs bank comparison

If you still aren't sure whether a Bank or Mortgage Broker is best for you, download my "Broker vs Bank Comparison" guide using the link below:

www.mortgageaustralia.com.au/brokervsbank

Case Study: why use a mortgage broker?

A recent MFAA / BankWest Home Finance Index showed that consumers saw clear benefits from using a mortgage broker.

Respondents listed the main benefits of using one:

- They do all the leg work for you (75.1% of respondents).

- They have a wider loan range (72%).

- They are experts in the range of mortgages from numerous lenders (71.1%).

- They can get the right loan for your circumstances (63.7%).

Forty-three per cent of recent or intending homebuyers say they would go to a Mortgage Broker to arrange a home loan, according to the MFAA / BankWest Home Finance survey, whilst thirty seven per cent of buyers in Australia still regard going direct to their own banks as their first preference.

The number of people preferring brokers has increased almost every year.

What exactly is a Mortgage Broker?

There are literally hundreds of different loan products available right now. While this makes it harder for you to choose the right loan, it also means that there's an ideal lending solution for you out there. It's just a matter of finding it.

That's where a Mortgage Broker comes in. A Mortgage Broker shops around for a loan that's right for you and your circumstances, whether you are a first-time homebuyer, looking to re-finance, building your investments, or looking for a competitive commercial finance product.

Mortgage brokers have access to hundreds of different loan products and they stay up to date with the constant changes and new products. This means that they are prepared to go to bat for you and match you with the right solution. A Mortgage Broker can also negotiate better rates on your behalf.

When is the best time to use a broker?

Wherever you are in the loan process, and whatever type of loan you're looking for, a broker can help. It doesn't matter the circumstance, whether you have just started thinking about buying, have already found the perfect house and want to quickly sort out your finances, are looking to unlock the equity in your current property, or want to find out if there's a better borrowing option than the one you currently have.

Any time is a good time to explore your options.

The first thing a broker does is meet with you to understand what it is you want. He is, after all, your personal finance professional, so the better a broker gets to know you, your financial circumstances and long term goals, the better he can match you with the product that's right for you.

Key Point

It's not just about finding the lowest interest rate; there are other things to consider. Let's say you're thinking about starting a family - so perhaps flexible repayments may be an important feature. If you want to renovate, easy access to equity can help. With so many products, you have so many choices.

Once you agree on the right loan, your broker will take care of the application and get everything in place for the approval process; then, see it through to settlement.

Why not just go to a bank?

It is hard for most people to choose which bank, which product. There are also building societies, mortgage managers and credit unions to consider. There are many options out there, and with the Reserve Bank of Australia moving official interest rates, and banks moving them independently, it's an ever-changing market. Not to mention all the new products and limited time special offers constantly being introduced.

> In the simplest terms, a Mortgage Broker makes things easy—saving you time and, in my experience, a whole lot of money.

With choice comes complexity. It can get tricky to navigate through it all. It can take much of your time (and sanity sometimes too).

A Mortgage Broker will steer you through this to find the loan that suits your needs, not the banks. He then deals with the lender and manages your application process through to approval. Because brokers save the bank's time and money by organising loans for them, the banks pay them for their time, you don't!

Example: does a mortgage broker cost more?

"But, surely using a broker must cost me more than going to the bank!"

Many people think that using a Mortgage Broker must cost them more. It makes sense that dealing directly with your own bank must cut out the middleman and ensure that you get a cheaper loan, right? Well, this is a common misconception of what brokers do and how your loan is organised.

Let's look at the facts:

Your bank is going to pay someone to organise your loan. Usually that is the lending manager at the branch, or their mobile lender who will come to your home.

Example *(cont.)*

Your broker will organise the exact same loan as the bank's own staff, and it won't cost you any more to use one.

A loan organised by a broker should cost no more for the bank than loans organised by their own staff.

That's because the bank doesn't have to pay the fixed costs of the broker's offices, salaries, cars and phones as they do with their own lending and administrative support staff. They only pay the broker if he successfully organises a loan for them. If your loan is declined, they don't pay the broker, but they still have to pay their own staff, regardless.

The key advantage to you, however, is that you have a much greater choice of lenders. It's fine to get the best loan your current bank can offer you, but it is less likely that your bank has the cheapest loan for your circumstances. A broker has 30 or more lenders to find the cheapest loan from.

Who can you trust to work in your best interests?

It's clear that a Mortgage Broker is more likely to have a cheaper loan than any individual lender, just through sheer weight of numbers. But what stops people, is knowing who they should trust, knowing who is really invested in them getting a cheap loan and paying it off quickly.

It is important to understand that a Mortgage Broker will limit their search to the lenders on their 'lending panel'. However, in most cases this will represent a very large proportion of the mortgage market. In the case of my company, around 90% of all home loans in Australia are with lenders on our lending panel.

A considerable amount of research goes into finding the best mortgage you might qualify for.

So much so, in fact, that it's not really practical for the average person to go to these lengths unless you have a lot of spare time on your hands. That's where a Mortgage Broker can come in very handy.

> By going the extra mile to research all the factors involved and find you the lowest cost product overall, a good broker can save you a heap of time, money and stress. They are like your private banker – with no allegiance to any particular bank.

Any reputable Mortgage Broker will recognise that getting the lowest cost loan they can for their customer and showing them how to pay it off fast is the best thing they can do – for their customer and for themselves.

The benefit to you in getting the cheapest loan your Mortgage Broker can organise is obvious, but what is the benefit to him?

When you pay off your home loan fast, you can start looking at buying investment properties and building wealth. This means more loans for your Mortgage Broker to organise, which is good for his business – but only if you were happy with his service and the low cost loans he organised for you in the first place.

Any halfway sensible Mortgage Broker understands that doing the right thing by his clients is the best way to get future loans, both for his current clients and also for their friends and family.

A Mortgage Broker's goal is to be your lending partner for life, without any allegiance to any particular lender. Most people get multiple home loans in their lifetime and it's in your Mortgage Broker's best interests to get their customers the best loans they can from their panel of lenders so they keep your trust to help you with your next loan.

I'm not saying there aren't bad or lazy Mortgage Brokers out there, but no more so than in any other walk of life. The nature of what we do in a very competitive industry is that if our customers aren't happy we won't stay in business very long.

Valuable Resource: mortgage broker checklist

Not all Mortgage Brokers are equal!

To help you quickly choose the right one, download my handy Mortgage Broker Checklist via the link below:

www.mortgageaustralia.com.au/brokerchecklist

Make sure your Mortgage Broker ticks off all the items in this checklist and you'll be confident they can get you a great loan – and avoid the pain of an expensive mistake.

CHAPTER 4

Don't shy away from smaller lenders

On the topic of hunting down the best loan, people often ask me whether it is safe to borrow with a smaller lender. The answer to that question is "Yes; because *you* have *their* money and not the other way around."

> Money is the same whomever you borrow it from; it's how much you have to pay back that matters.

Some borrowers worry about what might happen if their lender gets into financial trouble. Keep in mind again that *you* have *their* money—so don't worry too much. There are some smaller lenders whose names might not be readily familiar, but whose rates might be reason enough to get in touch and see what they have to offer.

Example: small lenders may save you big money

A 0.25% cheaper rate on a $300,000 home loan over 30 years is worth $43,536 in savings, which makes it well worth it to consider a lender you may not have heard of before.

The Australian mortgage industry is heavily regulated. Our lending practices are fairly conservative by world standards, as evidenced by our stability during the Global Financial Crisis (GFC). Small lenders have to

51

play by the same rules as the big lenders, and their loan contracts are the same, in my experience.

There really is no such thing as a hidden fee, not if you take the time to read your loan agreement.

In all cases, every lender must abide by the terms in their loan contracts, which must spell out every fee they can possibly charge you. If you have a concern, you should have a lawyer read over your loan contract.

The smaller players in any industry have to try harder to win your business because they don't have the advertising budgets or public profile that established businesses have. Consequently, they try to gain market share by offering more competitive products. In the case of lenders, this means cheaper loans.

The difference between banks and non-banks

Banks

$ Are authorised deposit taking institutions (ADI's) and can use their own funds to provide home loans.

$ They provide integrated banking packages including savings, transaction accounts, and credit cards.

$ Networks of branches provide additional service but contribute significantly to overhead costs.

$ The 'Big 4' banks are generally perceived poorly by the public and have low customer service ratings compared to their competitors.

Second-tier banks

$ There are a surprising number of household names beyond the 'Big 4' including ING Direct, Macquarie Bank, Suncorp, St George, Bank of Queensland, BankWest, Adelaide Bank, Citibank and AMP.

$ While some are now owned by the big banks it is worth considering their competitive offerings.

Building societies and credit unions

$ These non-profit cooperatives are owned by the people who use their services. Each member is both a customer and a shareholder.

$ Rates can be very competitive.

$ Member deposits are used to fund loans.

$ Like banks, they offer a wide variety of banking facilities with a focus on customer service.

$ They are regulated in the same way as banks.

Non-bank lenders

$ They do not hold an Australian banking licence so cannot accept deposits. They therefore source wholesale funding via investors, financiers, trusts and even the 'Big 4' banks.

$ Mortgage Managers are part of this group but rather than sourcing wholesale funds, they arrange finance for individual loans, lend it out under their own brand and perform a customer service role for the term of the loan on behalf of the underlying lender.

$ They do not have the overheads of an extensive branch or ATM network.

$ The appeal for customers has been lower interest rates, more flexible lending criteria (e.g. for low doc or non-confirming loans) and higher loan-to-valuation ratios (LVRs).

$ An emphasis on customer service, faster loan processing times and responsiveness are other selling points compared to the big banks.

$ Low rates are however often balanced by higher fees.

$ Clients are sometimes concerned about the financial security of these lenders, particularly with the potential of another global credit squeeze. Non-bank lenders may be less able to access funds and therefore more likely to pass on higher costs via interest rate rises.

$ They tend to have limited products and services so you might not be able to use them for all your financial needs.

One of my biggest frustrations is seeing borrowers regularly make the mistake of choosing a more expensive loan with a better-known lender.

Case Study: don't pay more for a brand name

Lender A—5.00%

Lender B—5.10%

Lender C—5.25%

Lender D—5.30%

On a $300,000 loan, Lender D costs $1,200 more every year than Lender A.

Lenders A, B, and C are smaller lenders that the customer hasn't heard of before, while Lender D is a discount package from a major bank that does a lot of advertising. Some people will choose Lender A, but many will choose Lender D, the most expensive one.

Lender D is still a very good loan; it's just not the best they can get. Put simply, the typical borrower is usually prepared to pay more to borrow money from a lender they are familiar with. In the finance industry, that usually means a lender that spends a lot on advertising.

As in every industry, there are companies who provide a less expensive product because they keep their advertising costs down, and those that provide a more expensive product but spend large sums on television advertising.

Key Point

When the product is money, the only thing you should be concerned about is the cost of borrowing that money, and the terms and conditions of that loan. If the terms and conditions of the loans are similar, choose the lower cost loan.

'Big 4' banks of Westpac, ANZ, NAB and the CBA are strong competitors with broad product ranges, so of course, you should turn to them if they have a solution that is suitable to your circumstances. However, you should feel just as good about choosing a second-tier bank or non-bank lender if their product, pricing, and services are better suited to you.

Ultimately the borrowing public is the winner due to a more competitive mortgage market. For borrowers, the biggest long-term negative effect of the Global Financial Crisis was that the 'Big 4' banks were allowed to buy up second-tier banks, which reduced competition in our industry and made smaller lenders all the more important.

A loan from a 'Big 4' bank may well be the best option for you. However, when choosing your next lender, please be open to other regulated credit providers you may not have heard of before if the loan they are offering is going to save you money; because, that is what really counts on your path to mortgage freedom.

Valuable Resource: lender information tip sheet

For a more detailed overview of the different kinds of lenders, download our info sheet now. Simply type the following into your web browser:

www.mortgageaustralia.com.au/beyondthebig4.pdf

STEP 3

Make sure your loan is always cheap

Once you have a cheap home loan, you can't assume it is always going to be the best you can get.

A home loan should not be a 'set and forget' proposition.

The third step to mortgage freedom is to keep a regular watch on better alternatives and special lending offers that will become available from time to time to make sure your own loan doesn't become overpriced by comparison (or the easy way is to get a mortgage professional who offers this service to do it for you).

Your goal is to futureproof your home loan, so it is always one of the cheapest you can get.

STEP 3

Make sure your loan is always cheap

CHAPTER 5

How to get a better deal

The single best way to *really* save money (and one of the easiest)

The Australian Government provides a great website aimed at helping consumers manage their money; it's called:

ASIC's **MONEYSMART**
Financial guidance you can trust

MoneySmart (<u>www.moneysmart.gov.au</u>)

According to the MoneySmart website — *"'Switching home loans could potentially save you thousands of dollars in interest or let you take advantage of features offered by another loan."*

In July 2011 lenders were banned from charging exit fees on home loans. Couple this with no mortgage stamp duty on your home loan which was charged in the past, and the government is making it the easiest it has ever been for borrowers to shop around for a better deal on a home loan.

At any given time, refinancing represents around a quarter of new home loans.

If shopping around for a loan frightens you, don't worry. I recommend going about it in a much simpler way; one that requires no financial discipline and can virtually be put on autopilot on your behalf, but we will discuss that at the end of this section.

A survey for Ernst & Young by Quantum Market Research found that 65% of borrowers were looking to be rewarded for loyalty with lower fees and better rates.

However, a third of potential switchers admitted that they gave up because there were too many choices to wade through and because the information was too complex. In other words, homeowners would like a better deal, but many of them find the hunt for one to be too hard or that they lack the time the hunt requires.

> It is vital that you keep assessing your financial needs and remain watchful for opportunities to get a better deal on your loan - or the easy way is to have someone do it regularly for you.

Getting a cheap loan is the first step, but monitoring it regularly to make sure you always have a cheap loan is the next step. Lenders are notorious for offering special deals and limited time offers for new borrowers, but not passing this onto existing customers. We regularly find clients with a loan taken out years ago with a lender where new clients have the exact same loan at a cheaper rate.

Is the grass greener on the other side?

So do you ever wonder if you are getting the best deal on your mortgage?

There is always fierce, ongoing competition between lenders in the home loan market, and the clear winner emerging from this constant battle is you.

> Even though you compared your options and secured the best deal a few years ago when you got your loan, that doesn't mean your interest rate is still the best you can do, or even close to it.

By refinancing with another lender, you could save money and get back a lot of time by paying your loan off sooner. Many borrowers who refinance are able to save as much as 1% off their interest rate, which could mean paying that loan off several years earlier than planned.

If you haven't reviewed your options for a while, it can pay to speak with your Mortgage Broker and find out if the grass really could be greener on the other side. It could make all the difference if you genuinely want to pay your loan off sooner and save money in the process.

Case Study: it pays to ask!

Here is a real home owner that a member of my team recently helped out.

We reduced their interest rate by 1.03%. This saved them a massive $23,115.77 every year for the life of their loan.

Not only that, we corrected the structure of their home and investment borrowings to also give them an annual tax deduction of $6,960 every year that they otherwise wouldn't have received.

Not everyone can get savings like this - the bigger your loan the greater the savings that can be achieved - but it's extremely rare that we don't produce a substantially cheaper setup for our clients.

As the Ernst & Young survey highlights, many borrowers believe they are currently getting a raw deal. According to the Australian Economic Record, Australian banks have passed on an average of 116% of each rate rise to their borrowers, but they only pass on 84% of each rate cut. This reluctance of lenders to pass on the full benefit of official interest-rate cuts to borrowers amplifies this "raw deal" sentiment.

Quite simply, the best reason to switch is to get a better deal, allowing you to pay your house off earlier. You might also consider refinancing so you can bundle your personal debts, such as credit cards, store cards, car loans, and personal loans, into your home loan. While this is usually a smart move—it will slash the amount you fork out in these other interest payments—it won't help you pay your mortgage off sooner unless you keep your repayments where they were across all your debts before the refinance.

Case Study: a good reason to switch

Here is another of many past clients we have helped.

We cut their interest rate by 0.55% by switching them to a new lender, in this case a discount offer from a Big 4 Bank. This reduced their monthly loan repayments by $458.33 for the life of their loan.

In fact, if they keep their repayments at the same level they were already paying them at; they will save $148,457 and be mortgage free 3 years and 9 months sooner. Or they may decide to use that money to start investing and build wealth for the future.

Either way, they are now massively better off and no longer throwing $458.33 away every month on pointless extra interest.

Let a mortgage broker take on the burden

You won't know if you can get a better deal until you start looking, which is when many people throw up their hands in surrender.

Talk to your Mortgage Broker first; we can very quickly answer your three most important questions:

1. Can I get a cheaper loan?

2. How long will it take?

3. How much will I save?

Your Broker can share insights about the broader home loan environment. Brokers deal with dozens of lenders and hundreds of loan products, so they have their finger on the pulse. In addition, they also have resources at their disposal that will take the heavy lifting out of the homework—the very reason that many homeowners claim that they can't be bothered to refinance.

Case Study: the power of expert negotiation

Here is another real client we have recently helped (names changed to protect their privacy):

Eric has been a self-employed electrician for 3 years while his wife Megan has worked in an administrative role for 6 years.

After seeing one of my team speak at a breakfast meeting about the benefits of having their interest rates reviewed regularly, Eric decided to call his bank. Being a client of theirs for 7 years he demanded a better interest rate than the 5.79% he was on.

A week later my broker spoke to Eric to see if he would like her to get a better deal for them.

He said not to worry as he had already done it himself and now had a rate of 5.13% - great news!!!

My broker then asked if he would mind if she could try with his lender and see if she could improve it further.

So with Eric's agreement she made a call to the lender and immediately over the phone got offered a rate of 4.75%.

Eric was furious at the bank for not offering the same rate to him so he booked an appointment and after reviewing his loans we looked at the structure and the way they handle their money, budget and ended up changing loans to a rate of 4.28% - a saving of $377.50 every month.

Happy campers!!!

CHAPTER 6
The real costs of refinancing

It's important that you understand, that while there *are* costs to refinance, they probably not nearly as much as you may think and are easy to work out before you go ahead.

In any comparison we do, we include these costs to give you a true savings figure. In most cases you should be saving a lot more than any one-off switching costs every single year of the new loan.

As I mentioned previously, Australian homeowners scored a win in 2011 when lenders were banned from charging exit fees on home loans, as part of the government trying to promote additional competition in the mortgage market.

If you are thinking of switching, you should make sure you get all the facts and compare like with like, so what you gain in the short term isn't lost in the long run.

There are however, a couple of situations where it is still usually best to wait before refinancing.

If you have a fixed rate

If you have a fixed rate it can be expensive to refinance as you will incur 'Break Fees'. Break fees on fixed rate loans are usually based on the interest rate you locked in compared to the current market interest rate, the length of time remaining on your fixed-rate term, and your original loan amount. They can run into thousands of dollars, and remain a formidable deterrent to fixed-rate customers thinking of refinancing.

In this case it is usually better to wait until the fixed rate expires and you have a variable rate again, at which time this fee no longer applies.

You can determine what the Break Fees will be by calling you lender and asking for a 'Payout Figure', then comparing this number to the amount you owe on your home loan. Make sure to confirm that the payout figure covers all the exit costs of the loan. If your payout figure is $278,000 but the amount owing on your loan is $272,000, then you know you have $6,000 in break fees and administrative costs to exit your loan.

Lenders mortgage insurance

The other thing to avoid is when you will get charged Lenders Mortgage Insurance when you are borrowing over 80% of the value of your home. Sometimes it is worth paying this fee because you will save more on a cheaper home loan, so it requires a case by case assessment.

Talking to your Mortgage Broker is one of the best ways to get a helicopter view of what it will cost you and what you stand to gain by refinancing.

Key Point

When refinancing, generally, you can expect to pay both a discharge and registration of mortgage fee of about $350 to $500 from your current lender, plus possibly an application fee of about $600 from your new lender.

Get the facts

One of the best ways to understand all of the pros and cons of a loan product is to ask the lender for a fact sheet. Many lenders don't offer fact sheets upfront, but they are now required to provide one if you ask.

Key fact sheets provide information in a set format so it's easier for you to compare loans. They also highlight important information, such as the total amount to be paid back over the life of the loan.

Beware of shrinking values

Sometimes property values will dip, so one of the trickier aspects of refinancing is knowing how much equity you have (the current value of your home, minus what you owe). If you bought just a few years ago and borrowed near or to your limit, you may find you have insufficient equity to secure a new loan or that you have to pay additional hefty charges in the form of Lenders Mortgage Insurance as I mentioned above.

If you already have Lenders Mortgage Insurance incorporated in your loan, you will have to take out a new policy with the new lender if you refinance.

If you need to borrow more than 80% of the value of a property, you will be charged Lenders Mortgage Insurance to cover the lender if you default on the loan. It can add thousands to a loan and, what's more, what you may have already paid won't be taken into account.

CHAPTER 7

Who should refinance?

Whether you make the switch or not always comes down to your circumstances. Critical factors include:

$ How much you owe on your existing loan and how long it will take to pay it off.

$ Your earning potential, now and in the future.

$ How long you plan to stay in your existing home.

$ Whether your living costs will increase in coming years (having children, for example).

Your Mortgage Broker is the best person to weigh up all of these factors, work out whether you should refinance, and then help you find the best new loan. They will also manage all of the paperwork to help make the refinance as simple as possible. People most often consider refinancing when they find themselves in one of these situations:

Found a cheaper rate

Have you ever thought: *"My lender is charging me a higher home-loan rate than I see advertised elsewhere. Can I change lenders?"*

This is the main reason most people change lenders and a broker can help you work out the potential savings.

When shopping around, a good start is look at the 'comparison rate' of each product. A comparison rate is essentially the 'true' rate, taking into account all fees and charges you will pay on the loan. There are limitations with a comparison rate, but it generally is a more accurate picture of a loan's cost that the advertised interest rate alone.

The honeymoon's over

"I have just come off a 'honeymoon' interest rate to a much higher rate. Can I move lenders or am I locked into my mortgage?"

In the past this may have been an issue as early repayment fees may have applied, but it is no longer legal to charge these.

Future rate rise worries

"If I move my mortgage to a new lender, is there anything stopping that lender from increasing their rates in a few months?"

It depends on the kind of product you have. If you're concerned about rising rates, perhaps you should consider a fixed-rate home loan, with fixed repayments for a period of 1 to 5 years. In my own experience however, people are usually better off in the long run sticking with variable rates. On a variable rate loan any lender can raise the rate at their discretion, it is extremely rare though, and you can just refinance out so it's not something lenders do if they want to keep their customers.

Why aren't they all equal?

"Why do some lenders charge more than others when lending the same amount of money?"

Banks and other lenders pay different amounts for the money they lend to you; they have different overhead structures and different profit expectations.

All these factors affect how much they charge to lend people money.

What could refinancing do for me?

Everyone knows that a home loan's interest rate is the most important factor in its overall cost. However, lower interest rates can save you very different amounts depending on how you pay your home loan.

Case Study: benefits of refinancing

The following comparisons are of a $300,000 home loan over 30 years at 6.4% compared to a loan that's 1% cheaper.

By refinancing at a lower rate, you could:

1) Save money every month

By reducing the interest rate by 1%, repayments go down by $192 per month. If you choose to pay these new lower repayments, you save $69,120 ($192 x 360 months) over the life of the loan.

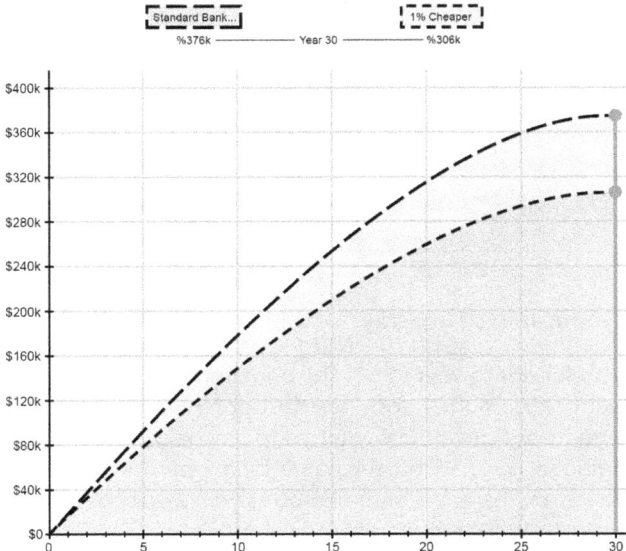

Case Study *(cont.)*

2) Cut years off your loan

However, if you maintain the repayments at the same amount as when you had the original, more expensive loan, because you have a lower interest rate, you are now paying off more of the principal every month ($192 more to be exact). This would have your mortgage paid off 6 years earlier, allowing you to avoid paying $111,948.31 in interest.

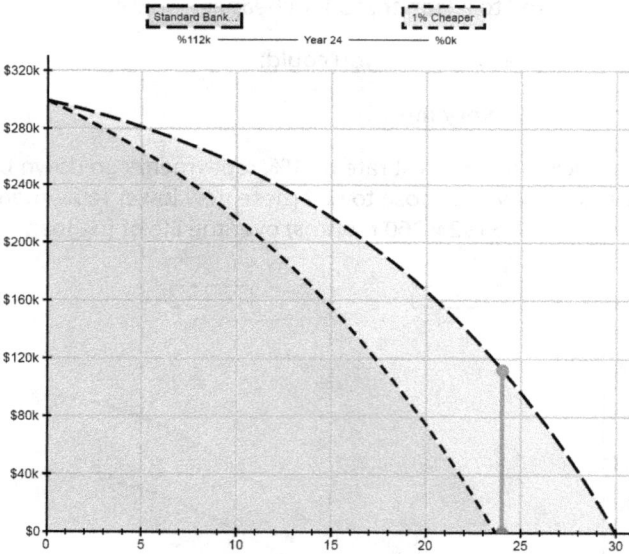

3) A big lump sum right away

If you prefer not to wait to get the benefit of the new, lower rate, if you want extra money right now but don't want to increase your repayments or the amount you had to pay back, you could borrow an additional $34,195 on the same loan when refinancing today and pay back the exact same amount you would have when the loan was at the 1% higher rate.

Case Study *(cont.)*

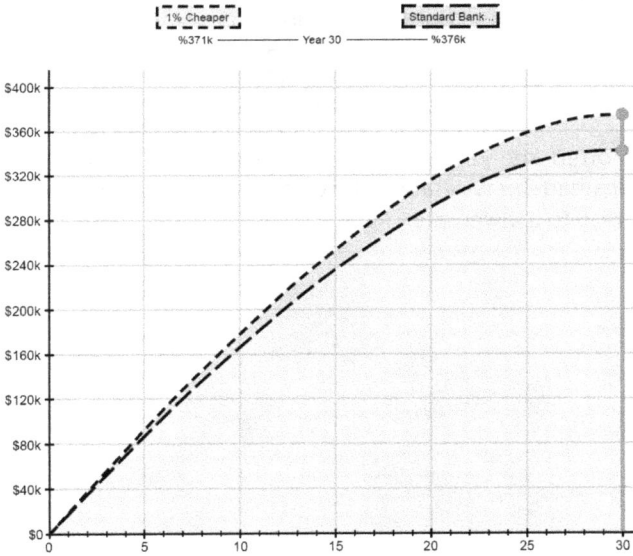

CAUTION: I do not advocate borrowing that extra money unless you are going to financially benefit from doing so in the long run. In general I recommend Option 2—paying your new, cheaper loan at the old, higher repayments.

It is worth understanding that $300,000 at 6.4% over 30 years is the same as borrowing $334,195 at 5.4% ($300,000 + the $34,195 you save by lowering your interest rate). You pay back the same amount on each loan, which is the real cost of the loan to you.

In this scenario, $34,195 is what you are giving away to the bank that you could have to spend today.

That's right, by choosing a lower interest rate, you could borrow $34,195 more right now and keep your repayments exactly as they are. This extra $34,195 is what you would have paid in interest to the more expensive

---

Case Study *(cont.)*

lender. The total you pay back will be exactly the same, but you would have an extra $34,195 right now to do whatever you want with!

It's not my suggested course of action with a cheaper loan, but the money is better in your pocket than the banks.

People often see refinancing as a hassle and are happy to plod along. Instead, be wise about just how much you could benefit from refinancing to a lower rate.

CHAPTER 8

Knowing when and how to get a cheaper loan

As a professional Mortgage Broker and Australian Credit Licensee, the most common question I am asked is: *"What's the best rate at the moment?"*

A better question to ask is: *"When is the **best time** for me to get the lowest cost loan I can?"*

The answer to this question is NOT *"When you are buying your first home?"* The CORRECT answer is *"When you have owned your current home for at least 12 months and have built up equity."*

A natural time for many homeowners to shop for the lowest cost loan is when they are selling their current home and buying their next one. They are already going to have to arrange a new mortgage, so it's a good opportunity to take advantage of the stronger position they are in compared to when they initially bought their current home.

When you buy your first home you are in your weakest borrowing position. You have no track record of home loan repayments and you have the least amount of equity.

This was certainly the case for me when I bought my first home, a 2 bedroom flat in Maylands, WA. I was happy to go with any lender that would help me with the small deposit I had and the First Home Owners Grant helping with fees.

Then as soon as you start to build some equity and a repayment history, you should be open to better alternatives. People often miss this and stick with their first home for many years and end up paying far more than they need to.

> ### ⊕ Key Point
>
> Equity matters because the more equity you have, the safer the bank sees you as, and you can access special rates.
>
> Having at least 12 months of repayment history proves you are a responsible person with a track record of meeting your commitments.
>
> The greater your equity grows and the longer your track record, the better.

When combined with Advanced Mortgage Reduction Strategies I'll discuss later in the book, you can really fast track your path to mortgage freedom by knowing when to refinance strategically.

> This is why a controlled-refinancing strategy, what I call "Future Proofing", is your simplest path to mortgage freedom (it is definitely not 'Set and Forget'). You can accomplish this by working with a trusted Mortgage Broker who will automatically monitor your home loan by periodically comparing it to more recent loan offerings.

At the very least it often means you can let your current lender know that you are aware of better loan options that you qualify for, and often they will try to match the deal to keep you as a customer.

For example, a bank customer was informed of an available loan option that would save them 0.65% compared to the existing bank loan. This customer raised this with their bank and got the same rate reduction applied to their loan.

Don't be complacent

The home loan market changes constantly; new lenders and new products are regularly introduced while old lenders and old types of loans frequently become superseded.

They rarely apply these better loan features or discounts to their existing home loans. Lenders regularly introduce cheaper versions of an existing loan or a new discount package to attract new borrowers.

Key Point

You should review your home loan at these key points:

$ At least every 2 years.

$ Whenever you come out of a fixed or introductory rate.

$ Whenever you believe an employment or income change is on the horizon.

$ When you are planning to have children.

$ When you are planning any major purchases.

$ When you are accumulating other debts, such as credit cards.

In my experience, the biggest financial problem people have is complacency. It all seems a bit too complicated, and it's much easier to just stick with your current loan. However, all the while, you are wasting money that you could be using to build your financial future.

Personally, I think an hour spent collecting a few papers and signing some forms is a small price to pay to save thousands of dollars (compare that to your hourly rate at work).

It can be simple to future proof your loan, especially when using a

Mortgage Broker, because:

$ When you get your first loan, your Mortgage Broker keeps all of your details securely on file.

$ Your Mortgage Broker contacts you when a new loan product they have already determined will genuinely save you a substantial amount of money is introduced, taking into account any exit and new setup costs.

$ Your Mortgage Broker already has your details, to get you started with these better options, he only requires an update of your details, some recent payslips, and loan statements.

$ Your Mortgage Broker can then create a prefilled application form ready for your signature.

$ Working with a broker takes all the time consuming work out of it for you.

Switching out of your current loan and taking out a loan at a lower rate can mean a difference measured in years and thousands of dollars. If you have a loan that is tricked up with all the features, or even if you have a standard variable loan, you might find that you could get a no frills rate that is as much as a percentage point cheaper than your current loan.

Set it on auto-pilot

Making it easier to become mortgage free is the primary focus of my Mortgage Broking company, Mortgage Australia. So completely free of charge, we regularly compare the current loans of our clients against the latest and cheapest home loan offers from our panel of dozens of major lenders, covering over 1,350 finance options.

Once you have a loan with us we conduct this review every 2-3 years (or at other milestones

such as when you exit a fixed rate) to ensure your existing loan is still one of the most competitive available. If not, we will provide you a savings comparison and you can decide if you wish to proceed. And because we have your details on our system it will be an even faster process to simply update them than your initial loan application with us was.

We will futureproof your loan, put on autopilot on your behalf.

⦿ Valuable Resource: your financial snapshot

The easiest way to get a great home loan now AND futureproof it, is to go directly to our 'financial snapshot' online form:

www.mortgageaustralia.com.au/snapshot

This short and easy form comes directly to me and gives me an overview of your financial situation so I can quickly see how we can help you.

Risk is a part of life. You take a risk when you get into a car or walk down the street. A friendly round of golf or sitting down for a meal involves risk, even if it's minimal. But using Mortgage Australia to get your next home loan means taking no risk at all! In fact, the risk is all ours.

If you meet with a Mortgage Australia Broker and we can't find a cheaper home loan than you currently have, we will pay you $1,000.00 to compensate you for your valuable time.

My belief is that if you can't guarantee the service you provide, you shouldn't be providing it.

Just complete our quick online financial snapshot to get started, knowing you are protected by our legally binding guarantee.

www.mortgageaustralia.com.au/snapshot.

MORTGAGE AUSTRALIA GROUP

$1,000.00
GUARANTEE

$1,000.00 Cheaper Home Loan Risk-Free Guarantee

100%
GUARANTEE

Mortgage Australia
MORTGAGE AUSTRALIA GROUP

Guarantee Reference Code RF458

Go to **www.mortgageaustralia.com.au/guarantee** for more details.

STEP 4

How to find the right, cheap home loan for you

Okay, so now you know the importance of getting a cheap loan and making sure it stays cheap, let's discuss a practical method for achieving this.

What you need is a way of comparing the true overall cost of the loan on an "apples to apples" basis, just like a reputable Mortgage Broker would do for their own home loan.

CHAPTER 9

Finding a *genuine* low-cost home loan

So how do you go about finding the lowest cost home loan available to you?

There are hundreds of home loan choices, and it can be overwhelming. It might be tempting to keep all of your banking in the same place for simplicity. Many borrowers apply with their current bank — definitely not the best way to get the cheapest loan.

Many homebuyers do not feel they have the time or the finesse to review all the possible loan options thoroughly. This is where it is a good idea to get a professional involved. A good Mortgage Broker knows the steps to take to get you the best loan product from their panel of lenders without causing you any extra stress.

In this chapter, we outline the 5-step process of finding a genuine low cost home loan deal; it takes some time to do this, but you should do it this way if you want to get it right. NOTE: if you or your trusted advisor is not doing this, you're flushing money down the toilet!

Step 1 - choose the right type of loan

The first thing to do is to get a solid understanding of the different types of loans.

> **◉ Valuable Resource: your guide to loan types**
>
> You can download our guide to the different types of loans from our webpage using the link below:
>
> **www.mortgageaustralia.com.au/loantypes**

Choosing a loan is about knowing what you need in the loan and talking with someone who can explain what it all means or doing your own research.

Step 2 - create a list of all major banks and lenders, and their products

Did you know that each lender might have up to 10 or more home loan products? These may include:

$ Standard home loans

$ Basic home loans

$ Professional packages

$ Lines of credit

$ Fixed rate term loans

$ Master limit loans

$ Portfolio loans

$ Capped home loans

$ Equity loans

$ Investment loans

Start with a list of at least 20 leading lenders, including the major banks. This results in a starting line-up of at least 200 products to compare. A typical Mortgage Broker will have over 30 lenders they work with at any given time, covering a wide cross-section of lender types and loan options. They should be up to date with all their latest special offers and lending policies.

👁 Valuable Resource: lenders we've worked with

Since 2000, Mortgage Australia has settled over $3 Billion in Home Loans, and has worked with these lending institutions:

ANZ	Illawarra Mutual Building
Adelaide Bank	Society
AFG Home Loans	ING Direct
AMP Bank	Integris Home Loans
Bank of China	Keystart
Bank of Melbourne	La Trobe Financial
Bank of Queensland	Liberty Financial
Bank SA	Macquarie Bank
Bankwest	Mariner
Bluestone	Maxis Loans
Capital Finance	Members Equity Bank
Citibank	MKM Capital
Collins Securities	Mortgage Ezy
Commonwealth Bank	Mortgage Mart
Deposit Power	Mortgage Street
GE Money	National Australia Bank
Heritage Bank	National Mortgage Market
Home Building Society	Corporation
Homeloans Limited	Now Finance
Homeside Lending	Over Fifty Group
HSBC	Pepper Homeloans
RAMS	Police and Nurses Bank
RBS	The Rock Building Society Ltd
RHG	Think Tank
St George Bank	Westpac
Suncorp Bank	Wide Bay Australia

Find us at **www.mortgageaustralia.com.au** or **Freecall 1800 180 800**

Step 3 - choose an appropriate term over which to compare loans

When searching for the ideal home loan, look for the best deal over a 5 year term (taking into account interest and all charges). For most people, 5 years is around the time a change takes place, with either the home or the loan.

Always consider that lenders are constantly coming out with new products, specials, and policies that can save borrowers large amounts of money. In practice, a better deal is very likely to come along within the 4 to 6 year time span, making the 5 year mark a good point of comparison.

Step 4 - choosing the features you want

You definitely want a loan that allows you to make lump-sum repayments to try to get the loan paid off earlier, as well as a redraw facility to take out extra payments if you need to. An Offset Account can be very useful if you don't need to pay a higher rate to get it (the correct method for using one I will discuss later).

Make a list of any other features that are important to you and remove any of the loans that don't have the features you need. Remember, different loans have different purposes, so you need to match a loan to your needs.

Discarding the loans that have features you don't need may save you 1% or more on the interest rate. If you do that for every loan you have for the next 30 years, that's a whole lot of money you've just saved yourself.

Don't take a standard loan when it will cost you more in interest. Whatever features you want are probably available at a cheaper rate. A professional Mortgage Broker with a focus on a loan you pay off fast can make this process easy by helping you quickly identify the loan features that are going to be most relevant to you and finding the lenders that don't charge a premium to access them.

👁 Key Point

Don't get hung up on fees. While you want a loan with as few fees as possible, you need to take into account the total cost of the loan. You are better off paying a $10 monthly fee than an extra $15 a month in interest. A 'fee free' loan may sound great but may not be all is cracked up to be when you do a proper comparison.

Step 5 - calculate total costs as a percentage of the loan value.

Once you have a shortlist of lenders whose lending criteria you meet and whom appear to be very competitive, divide all their costs (interest and fees) into 5 years and come up with a percentage. The lender with the lowest percentage gets your business.

🗄 Case Study: comparing loans

Let's compare "**Loan A**" and "**Loan B**" (in practice, there would be dozens loan products included from the lender panel in this comparison, but this is just for illustration purposes).

	Loan A	Loan B
Loan amount	$350,000	$350,000
Interest rate	6.00%	5.95%
Application fee	$395	$0
Annual fee	$0	$395
Settlement fee	$0	$220
Valuation fee	$0	$250
Legal fee	$0	$150

Case Study *(cont.)*

Lenders mortgage insurance	$7,500	$9,500
Loan discharge fee	$350	$350
Total cost over 5 years	$113,245	$114,990
Avg. annual rate over 5 years (true cost)	**6.47% pa**	**6.57% pa**

In this example, the loan with the higher interest rate (Loan A) actually works out to be effectively 0.10% per annum cheaper every year for 5 years.

Choosing the right lender

The lender you choose often determines just how effective all the above steps are.

Every bank calculates their loans in different ways. Some accept certain forms of income (such as family allowance payments, casual income, etc.) while others do not. Some banks assume different amounts when working out your living expenses and how much disposable income you have. They also look differently at any existing loans and credit cards you may have.

Key Point

Each bank has its own "Assessment Rate". They don't usually assess how much you can borrow based on the interest rate you will be borrowing on; instead, they use a higher interest rate to allow for future rate changes.

This is important to know because if you apply to a lender and get knocked back, it makes it harder to get approved with the next lender because it leaves a record — a 'credit enquiry' - on your credit file. This is because when the next lender sees it, particularly if there are a lot of credit enquiries on your record, they become concerned as to why other lenders are declining your application or think you are a reckless borrower, which counts against you.

Not only that, banks also frequently change their affordability calculations depending on their own internal requirements. They often intentionally reduce or increase the amounts their customers can borrow. In fact, depending on the type of loan you choose, you can often borrow a different amount from the same lender.

For all of these reasons, it is important to cautiously choose the right lender for you and your situation.

Valuable Resource: have an expert help you

Don't forget, the above steps can all be done for you, free of charge, by a reputable Mortgage Broker using the lenders on their panel, who understands your goal of becoming mortgage free and who knows the lenders most likely to approve your loan.

To have a professional on your side, just send me an email and I will have one of my expert team complete this process for you from over 1,350 finance options.

davidham@mortgageaustralia.com.au

Remember, there is no cost for this service. It's easy, we do all the work – and you could save lots of money.

CHAPTER 10

Are you getting the discount you deserve?

All banks offer a Standard Variable loan. This is usually a fully featured loan at a rate that's around 0.5% higher than their Basic Variable rate. Lenders have always given introductory or honeymoon discounts on this Standard Variable rate, but just for the first year of the loan.

Years ago they began giving permanent discounts based on what they considered stable and profitable professions—typically to Doctors, Lawyers, and Accountants. In fact, these discounted loans are often still referred to as "professional packages".

> ### ⊙ Key Point
>
> Some lenders offer packages which are branded to different industry groups, such as teachers or nurses. It is important to know that just because a loan has the name of your industry on it, it does not mean it's the cheapest loan you can get. This is usually a savvy marketing ploy by a lender to get you to take a mental shortcut and assume this is a better offer because it is 'tailored' to the needs of your profession.
>
> In reality I typically find that whilst these loans are an improvement on the bank's standard loans, cheaper alternatives are readily available, often with the same lender. Certainly consider these options, but no more than any other loan you are comparing – always look at the final cost.

Virtually every lender offers a discount package that most of their borrowers are eligible for. These packages go by many different names, including "Wealth Package", "Advantage Package", "Breakfree", "Wealth Plus", "Mortgage Advantage", "Choice Package", and many more.

In more recent years, as well as these professional packages, discounts have been based on the amount that people borrowed—the larger the loan the bigger the discount. Different lenders offer very different discounts at different loan amounts. Since the Global Financial Crisis, a new category of discount loan has emerged—I call them "Safe Borrower" loans.

When you organise a loan through a reputable broker, they will know all of the discount packages you are entitled to and determine which is the cheapest loan overall. They can make sure you get the best discount package you qualify for that your current lender may not be telling you about.

If you aren't borrowing enough to be eligible for a discount package or don't fall into the right profession, don't worry, there is in recent years a new type of discount package – one that makes it all the more important to keep reviewing your lending options as I've described previously.

What is a Safe Borrower?

A Safe Borrower to a bank is like a Safe Driver to an insurance company; you are low risk because you have a proven history.

When you are a first homebuyer with no repayment history and a small deposit, probably using the First Home Owners Grant to pay your fees, the bank looks at you like an 18-year-old behind the wheel of a V8: high risk and unproven. If you are a Safe Borrower, the bank sees you as experienced, with a history of accident-free driving.

A new focus - LVR

The LVR, or Loan to Value Ratio, is an important principle to understand when discussing Safe Borrowers.

An LVR of 100% means someone is borrowing 100% of the value of the property, such as a $300,000 loan on a $300,000 house. Similarly, a 50% LVR means a $150,000 loan on a $300,000 house. The 50% LVR is much safer for the lender because, if the borrower has a problem, they can comfortably sell the house for much more than the loan.

> ### Key Point
> Interest rates for Safe Borrowers are usually more than 1% lower than the bank's standard variable rates, cheaper even the bank's lowest advertised discount and professional package rates. Think of it like the No-Claim Bonus on your car insurance.

Are *you* a Safe Borrower?

Ask yourself these 3 questions:

1. Do you have a perfect repayment history on your existing home loan for at least the last 6 months?

2. Do you owe less than 75% of the value of your home – the lower the better (e.g., less than $375,000 on a home valued at $500,000)?

3. Have you been working for the same employer for at least 1 year or have you been in continuous employment or self-employed for 2 years in the same industry?

If you answered 'Yes' to all these questions, the banks consider you a very low risk customer. If so, you shouldn't be paying the same interest rate as an unproven borrower.

Why do banks need Safe Borrowers?

Just like everyone has a personal credit rating, all banks and lending institutions have a credit rating too. That credit rating is very important when they obtain funding for the money they lend as a home loan. If the bank has a low (poor) credit rating, they pay a higher price for their funding, which, in turn, means a more expensive loan for you.

A major component of a bank's credit rating is the combined risk profile of all their home loans. If a bank's total home loans are very high when compared to the total value of the homes they were lent for, this is considered risky. If a bank has lent to too many people who didn't provide financial information or many first-home buyers, this is also considered risky. This is also why banks charge Mortgage Insurance to borrowers with a small deposit, to protect themselves against high LVR loans. Banks need to keep this risk profile down by attracting low risk customers.

So isn't it fair that if you are helping the bank reduce its costs, you should also save?

How to take advantage of being a Safe Borrower to be mortgage free years earlier

If you aren't already a Safe Borrower, you will be one in the future by maintaining an orderly repayment history as you build equity in your home. Just don't expect your bank manager to call you up and offer you a cheaper rate when you get there, you'll need to ask for it or get your Mortgage Broker to find out which you qualify for.

Even if you aren't already a Safe Borrower, you can still take advantage of special lending offers. Lenders typically promote a "Standard" rate loan through their advertising and on their websites.

Always investigate the discounts your lender offers. Every day, people who have had loans with their bank for years have missed out on taking advantage of discount packages they were eligible for. They end up paying thousands in extra interest.

> ### ⊕ Key Point
>
> Claiming your status as a Safe Borrower pays off because a discount of a 1% lower interest rate saves you $159,559 in interest on a $300,000 home loan.

The discounts offered in these packages vary widely, as do the standard rates the lenders offer. Usually, the discounts range from 0.3% to 1%; sometimes more, sometimes these discounts are applied only to the variable rate, but sometimes also to the lender's fixed rates.

Eligibility for the discount is also based on the amount you are borrowing. Larger loans typically qualify for larger discounts. The discount package may require you to take out a credit card with a minimum limit or open an additional account with the lender.

Discounts for larger loans

As I've mentioned, lenders often offer a better rate for a large loan, for example, 0.9% or more off the Standard Variable Rate instead of 0.7%. That extra 0.2% can make a BIG difference.

Some lenders may charge a $600 application fee but waive it if the loan is over a certain amount. Some lenders are able to access discretionary and 'private banking' pricing, where they will actually make special offers to win quality loans.

> 💡 Lenders CAN be persuaded to sweeten their terms, if you know the right questions to ask.

If you still can't get a discount - try this!

If you aren't borrowing enough or don't meet your lender's other requirements to qualify for a discount, I generally recommend a basic, variable rate.

A discount loan is a bank's standard loan with a reduced interest rate. The discount loan usually has an Offset Account or direct payment feature, which the basic loan doesn't. However, in most cases it is worth it to take the basic loan, which should have an interest rate similar to the discount loan, but without a few bells and whistles.

Certainly, I would almost always suggest that you take a basic loan if you can't get a discount off the standard loan. This is because the additional features of the standard loan are rarely worth the higher interest rate compared to a basic loan, which is usually 0.5% cheaper, and that equates to $1,500 per year on a $300,000 home loan.

As long as the basic loan allows you to make extra repayments, you probably aren't missing out on too much by choosing it. Basic and cheaper is almost always better than fully featured and more expensive.

> Without a compelling reason to do otherwise, choose the lowest cost loan.

Many lenders offer fantastic basic loans these days with very few restrictions; so, if your lender only offers you a standard rate, be sure to ask to see their full list of loan offers.

Valuable Resource: are you eligible for a discount?

Speak with a Mortgage Australia Broker to find out the discount loans you are eligible for. Just let them know you have read 'The 7 Easy Steps to Mortgage Freedom' and they will know how to help you.

Visit **www.mortgageaustralia.com.au** to find your local broker who is trained in the processes described in this book or **Freecall 1800 180 800** and you will be automatically connected to your closest Mortgage Australia Broker.

Remember, we do not charge for our services.

STEP 5

Avoid these mortgage traps

Okay, so now we know how to get a cheap loan with any discounts available to us. And we know that the longer we are in our loan that further discounts may become available as we build equity and become more valued by our bank due to our lower lending risk profile.

The fifth step is making sure to avoid the most common mortgage mistakes. Individually or in combination, they can be a major stumbling block to your goal of mortgage freedom.

The traps are out there — so you must know what they are and how to avoid them!

Your bank is very happy when you do the things I'll describe below, because they all add up to keeping you in your home loan longer.

CHAPTER 11

Avoid the debt consolidation trap

Consolidating your debts to a lower single repayment is usually a good idea, as long as it is done the right way and as long as you don't do it over and over again.

The lowest interest rate loan you are likely to have is your home loan. Personal loans, car loans, credit cards and store cards will almost always be at a much higher interest rate. It is very attractive and financially sensible to increase your home loan to pay out those debts and then have one single lower monthly payment to think about, as long as you avoid these traps.

Trap 1 – paying the new minimum repayment

Personal and car loans usually have a 5-7 year loan term. When you pay them out with your home loan (i.e. consolidate) you are borrowing money over a 30 year period. As a result you may end paying a lot more interest than you would have.

Example: minimum repayment trap

Let's say you owed $10,000 on a 12% personal loan over 5 years. Your repayment would be $223 per month and you would pay a total of $3,344 in interest over the 5-year term.

If you decided to consolidate this personal loan by increasing your home loan by $10,000 at 6% and paying the personal loan out, your new home loan repayment would increase by only $60 per month.

On the surface that looks great – because $223 minus $60 is an extra $163 in your pocket each month.

But here's the trap: if you did only pay this new minimum repayment, you would end up paying $11,596 in interest – or $8,252 MORE. This is because you are now paying the personal loan over 30 years instead of 5 years.

So if you do pay out other debts with your home loan, keep your repayments where they were already.

In this example, if you kept paying $223 per month (instead of the $60 per month extra which is the minimum requirement) you would end up saving $1,354 in interest on the personal loan and pay it off 8 months sooner.

Trap 2 – taking on more debt

When you consolidate your debts you will see your repayments fall and extra money in your pocket every month. Don't be tempted to start borrowing again just because you now feel you can afford it.

This happens a lot with credit cards. People get in over their heads in credit card debt (very easy when the bank keeps sending out limit increases), so they add this debt to their home loan to get themselves out of trouble. But old habits take over and the credit cards start rising again – it's a downward spiral that could trap you in debt indefinitely!

Key Point

To avoid both these traps, keep your repayments up to where they were before you repaid or consolidated your other loans. Instead of falling behind you will accelerate your home loan and get the best outcome.

Your goal – build both your equity *and* your cash flow

Becoming mortgage free faster means that you need to grow the equity you have built up in your home – this is because you will later use the equity you have built up to create additional sources of cash flow to accelerate repaying your home which I will discuss later.

But if you have a lot of other debts your cash flow will be lower which will make it harder to build equity in the first place. For this reason it is usually worthwhile sacrificing some equity by consolidating your debts to improve your cash flow so you can then pay your loan down faster.

For many people the first thing we do is consolidate their debts into a single, cheaper home loan which frees up hundreds of dollars a month. Then we look at directing that extra money into the new home loan. In that case they are definitely better off and moving much faster to becoming mortgage free. But if they start using the extra money to borrow on their credit cards again, this is the opposite of becoming mortgage free.

If you start treating your home loan like an ATM you'll be going backwards.

CHAPTER 12
Other mortgage traps to avoid

Regardless of whether or not you opt to work with a Mortgage Broker or not for your next home loan, it is prudent to know the types of loans to be cautious of.

A little warning for you—if it sounds too good to be true, it probably is.

When shopping for a mortgage, it's important to consider which features you need in a loan:

$ Do you want to be able to make extra repayments when times are good?

$ Would you like to be able to take that money back again if something doesn't go according to plan?

$ What about if you want to change your repayment frequency?

Key Point

The features of your loan can be just as important as the interest rate— and not paying attention could mean that you end up paying much more in the long term.

When it comes to choosing the right loan for you, there are a few things to watch out for; some may even be 'financially fatal' traps that you will want to avoid. The excitement of buying your next home can be all too distracting. If you are not mindful, putting your foot in one of these traps can be easy, especially if you neglect to research your loan options.

The 'where is the branch?' trap

Does it really matter if your lender doesn't have branches for you to walk into?

The reality is that if they have a physical branch you are very likely paying more for the privilege. In an age where everything you need to do with your home loan can be done online or over the phone, you have to ask what value the expense of a branch is giving you.

If it costs your lender money to maintain and staff a branch, that cost will be reflected in your loan.

In the same way, don't be concerned about having your home loan with a different institution than the one you do your banking with. For most people when their home loan is set up they simply use internet banking to keep track of it and make any extra repayments or redraws. You can still use a bank with branches for your banking.

The honeymoon trap

One of the most common mortgage traps, the honeymoon loan, often seems like a wonderful offer on the surface: "Low introductory rate for the first 12 months". If you're buying your first home, you might imagine this to be a great way to ease into home ownership without being hit too hard by the loan repayments.

However, just as Christmas always comes around sooner than you think, so too does the end of the honeymoon period. For many borrowers who haven't done enough homework, this anniversary can bring very bad tidings in the form of a whopping repayment increase.

⊕ **Key Point**

Beware of lenders bearing gifts and skip the honeymoon.

Introductory, or honeymoon rates have long been an important marketing tool for lenders. They initially offer you a cheap rate on your loan to get you in the door, but once the honeymoon period is over, your loan switches to a higher variable rate of interest.

There are two problems with this scenario:

1. First, the later variable rate is usually higher than some of the available lower basic loans are, so you end up paying more.

2. Second, you need to clearly understand that a honeymoon rate applies only for the first year or two of the loan and is a minor consideration compared to the actual variable rate, as that rate will determine your repayments over the next 20 or so years.

💡 When tempted with one of these loans, consider what you will do at the end of the honeymoon, when you suddenly have to come up with an extra $400 or so per month.

This tactic is such an issue that the government introduced mandatory "Comparison Rates" to combat the often misleading advertising associated with honeymoon rates. When I compare loans, I present the True Rate of the loan, which takes into account any introductory rates and ongoing fees. In some cases an introductory rate can be worthwhile; especially if you plan to have land for only a short period of time or if the loan reverts to a competitive rate after the honeymoon. Just make sure you fully understand what you are getting yourself into before setting off on a "honeymoon" with your lender. Before jumping headfirst into an attractive introductory rate loan, make sure you take the time to compare the 'post introduction' rate with other loans on the market. At the end of the day, what really counts is how much you will pay for the other 29 years of the loan. After all, choosing an expensive loan product can really impact your ability to achieve your financial goals.

The fees and charges trap

Loan contracts can be very detailed, packed full of confusing words and legal disclaimers. One section that you should study with a magnifying glass is the 'schedule of fees and charges':

- $ Make sure you know whether you can make changes to your repayments.

- $ Find out how much it will cost if you default on a repayment.

- $ Are there fees associated with ordering a statement ahead of time?

- $ Most importantly, what establishment fees will you have to pay at the settlement of the loan? If you don't know this amount, you might not be able to proceed with your purchase and you could lose your deposit.

> It is critical that you take the time to research the different loan options available to you, and ask plenty of questions to ensure that the loan you choose is the best option for you.

The government 'Comparison Rates' trap

The government originally mandated 'Comparison Rates' as a way to make it easier for consumers to compare the true cost of a loan. But here's the trick you may not have realized.

Key Point

The Comparison Rate actually smooths out the appearance of any large fees charged in the first 5 years, presenting them over a 25-year period. The large fees are still there, they just don't look so astronomical when looked at over the life of the loan.

Keep in mind that the average home loan only runs 4-6 years before changing to another product or moving to another lender. In fact, the first 5 years tend to be where the real cost accrue, as the home owner buys, sells, upgrades, downgrades, redraws for a holiday, renovates, consolidates debt, or refinances for a better deal.

Because of this, many lenders will stack their fees at the front end of the loan, knowing full well that they will be hidden by the 25-year Comparison Rate. This makes their high cost (i.e. highly profitable) loans look 'cheap'. Because of this, the government no longer legally requires Comparison Rates to be displayed.

Loans to avoid

Particularly avoid Bridging Finance and 'Standard Loans'.

Bridging finance

Bridging finance is a loan you get to buy your next home while you are trying to sell your current home. The lender 'allows' you to skip paying interest on it and just keeps adding it to the loan amount.

If you don't sell your home as quickly as you think you will, you can end up with a much bigger loan than you started with. It also puts extra pressure on you to sell at a lower price than you might want.

It's much more prudent to be patient and know your home is sold before borrowing for your next one. Easier said than done I know, but there is nothing worse than sitting on a bridging loan for a year and finally being forced to sell at a price you didn't want.

Standard loans

You should really never take out a 'Standard Variable Rate' loan with a bank. There are plenty of discount packages available that lenders apply to their Standard Variable loans. If you don't qualify for a discount package then it usually means you should just take a Basic loan instead, as you probably won't benefit from the extra features a Standard Loan may have offer at a higher price.

The fixed-rate trap

You might be tempted to lock in a low interest rate for a couple of years so that you can have the peace of mind that comes with always knowing what your repayments will be.

In my experience over the term of your loan you are very unlikely to be better off fixing your rates. You might win in the short term, but the odds are against you.

Key Point

The danger here, though, is that you may be missing out on other important features, particularly the ability to make extra repayments or repay the loan early without a substantial penalty.

I'll talk more about my reasoning behind this and the decision between fixed and variable rates, particularly as it relates to our goal of becoming mortgage free faster, in the next chapter.

CHAPTER 13
Fixed or variable?

One of the main choices you need to make early on is whether to opt for a variable or fixed rate loan.

In general, if your goal is becoming mortgage free faster, a variable rate loan is a better option. Everyone needs to assess their needs on a case-by-case basis, but in general, the flexibility of a variable loan has the advantages of allowing us to more easily refinance to a better deal, and more options for extra repayments.

Having said this, some lenders offer fixed rates with an Offset Account, which I will detail the advantages and proper use of later in this book. A fixed rate loan with an Offset Account effectively does allow you to make extra repayments, but you still can't pay the loan out entirely without incurring break fees.

Be careful with fixed-rate loans

Fixed rates are generally based on what the economy is expected to do over the next few years, while variable rates are more aligned to the current cash rate, set by the Reserve Bank of Australia.

So if fixed rates are lower than variable rates the banks are expecting interest rates to fall. Therefore if the bank's highly paid economic forecasters are right, then fixing won't benefit you because variable rates will drop anyway.

Conversely, when fixed rates are higher than variable rates the banks are expecting interest rates to rise. So again, if the bank's economists are right, then fixing still won't benefit you because you had to take a higher fixed rate as rates rose.

Also, the longer the fixed rate term the higher the rate. This is because the further into the future you look the more difficult it is to predict the economy. So the banks build themselves in a greater safety margin.

> For these reasons borrowers are on average usually worse off when they fix rates. Of course, not always, and you need to look at how the specific loan offer compares and your personal situation, but in general the odds are against you saving money over the long term by fixing your rate.

There are reasons for taking out a fixed loan, but I'd recommend against doing it on the basis of predicting where interest rates are going. Even if you do pick it right and rates rise, you will only have a temporary reprieve until the fixed rate expires. And what often happens then is that you fix again at the higher rate, then variable rates fall and you lose out.

Of course, the decision between fixed and variable should take into account your personal situation and you should make up your own mind. Interest rates will fluctuate and you need to be confident you can afford higher rates if they rise.

Where fixed rates *are* useful is that they allow certainty in terms of repayments and can give you confidence when you feel you can't afford a rate increase. So they do have their place in the right circumstances. But as a method for becoming mortgage free faster, I believe they bring too many restrictions.

Valuable Resource: guide to loan types

For a more detailed look at the different types of loans and their pro's and con's, download my free loan guide from the following website:

www.mortgageaustralia.com.au/loantypes

STEP 6

Smarter money management

Now that you know how to sidestep these mortgage traps, the sixth step is to make sure you have your finances organised in the most productive way.

CHAPTER 14

Good debt vs bad debt

Next I'd like to discuss one of the fundamental principles of mortgage freedom and building wealth - namely, good debt and bad debt.

Most people think that *all* debt is bad. Most people have been taught that owing money is not a good thing and we should pay it off as quickly as possible. In most cases that is correct, but a home loan is just a tool, and like any tool it can be used the right and way and the wrong way.

> Prudent debt, when used properly and sensibly, is the fastest way to grow personal wealth.

It is this understanding that has made a huge difference in my own path to mortgage freedom.

Bad debt

Simply put, this is debt that costs you money. Most people borrow money to buy things that they use, but that don't provide them an income, such as a holiday, car (for personal use) and even your home. These are all good things to have, some you would argue are essential to have, but they all take money from you.

> Bad debt should be prioritised in order of the interest rate or overall cost of that loan and paid off as quickly as possible.

Based on this definition, your home loan is 'bad debt' and therefore should be paid off as quickly as you can - but as you build up equity you can start to turn the asset that is your home into a source of 'good debt', which is going to accelerate your journey to mortgage freedom.

Some people think they can avoid major debt by renting and never buying a home. However I would also classify paying rent as a form of bad debt. It is a debt you owe your landlord each month (and all your future landlords).

⊕ Key Point

Whether you pay rent or a home loan, you are still paying a large sum of money over your lifetime, but with a home loan you have a house that you own at the end as opposed to helping your landlord pay off their home.

Good debt

This is debt that you have used to buy assets that generate income for you that is greater than the cost of the debt.

💼 Example: what is good debt?

If you borrow money at 6% per annum and you invest in something that pays you 7% per annum, that is 'good debt' – because you have made more money than it cost you to borrow.

The interest on good debt is usually tax deductible. Obviously, you need to be conscious of the stability of the income and the asset you have purchased, and obtain any tax and financial advice from a specialist, but the principle is clear. For most people, the safest way to do this is through investing in property, which again should be done with help from experts and after taking the time to thoroughly educate yourself.

The most important thing is to avoid growing your bad debt.

Instead focus on paying it down quickly which will give you the chance to build up good debt over time, which in turn is the income you can then use to boost the speed at which you reduce your bad debt. And then you will have more money for the good things in life!

Unfortunately, whilst most people understand the need to avoid bad debt, they are less informed about the importance of making debt work for you.

Using equity to turn bad debt into good debt

Equity is the difference between the current value of your property and the amount you owe the lender. If you have already paid off some of your home, you have equity because you owe less than the value of the property.

Case Study: smart use of your equity

Using your equity is the real key to racing towards mortgage freedom.

If you have a property worth $500,000 on which you owe $150,000, you have equity of $350,000.

Lenders will allow you to borrow using your equity as collateral. Most lenders will allow you to borrow as much as 90% of the loan-to-value ratio (LVR) of your available equity (although I don't recommend being nearly this aggressive).

If you are careful, you can use this equity to your advantage to pay off your home loan sooner. Larger expenses, such as cars and holidays that would have been paid by credit card, are less costly on the lower rate of your home loan. So you can use your equity to reduce your other, more expensive debt - and then use the overall savings to accelerate your home loan.

Case Study *(cont.)*

Most loans allow you to consolidate (re-finance) all of your debt under the umbrella of your home loan. This means that instead of paying 15-20% on your credit card or personal loan, you can transfer these debts to your home loan and pay it off at a fraction of that cost.

As always, any extra repayments or lump sums will benefit you in the long run.

However, as I've spoken about already, please don't fall into the trap of consolidating your debt into your home loan and then incurring more debt on your newly paid out credit cards. It is usually worthwhile to bring all your debt to its lowest possible interest cost, but doing it over and over again will cost you dearly in the long run.

When you pay your debt down faster you can now use your growing equity to start switching your bad debt to good debt. Simply stated—bad debt costs you money, while good debt makes you money. The key to financial freedom is understanding this and applying it to your life. When all your debt is good debt, life is much easier and financially more secure.

To be clear, I am not a financial advisor. I hold an Australian Credit Licence, which allows me to help people compare and choose loans. But I can explain the general concepts and difference between 'Good and Bad Debt' and let you draw your own conclusions. I also suggest you seek financial advice specific to your situation from a licensed advisor.

CHAPTER 15

Get some free financial education

By world standards, Australia is a wealthy nation. We have a strong economy, a high employment rate, and a far rosier outlook than most developed countries. Yet, almost half (47 percent) of us are anxious about our finances, according to research by the Boston Consulting Group. In large part I think this is because people don't have a good handle on where their money is going, so it's difficult to feel in control.

I mentioned the government's MoneySmart website previously, which is a great, free resource which can help. I believe everyone should spend some time on the site, particularly with their children to help them develop good money habits early on. That is why I am part of the financial group that sponsors 'MoneySmart Week' each year.

The Federal Government's MoneySmart program has created a handy online tool for anyone in need of a financial health check. The aim is to help Australians be more financially resilient for the long haul.

> **Valuable Resource: how are your finances?**
>
> To find out how your finances are faring, take a Money Health Check online at the MoneySmart website using the link below:
>
> **www.moneysmart.gov.au/tools-and-resources/calculators-and-tools/money-health-check**

The Money Health Check helps you get back to basics by looking at your circumstances and financial goals and helping you develop strategies to reach them. The questions are straightforward and prompt you to consider some financial red flags you may not be aware of, or that you perhaps prefer to ignore!

There are also tools to help individuals and household's budget, set saving goals, and calculate their net worth. If you are like me, you know that a dollar saved is a dollar earned (in fact, it's even more valuable because you don't pay tax on it!). We all spend a lot of time trying to find the best prices on our day to day essentials—groceries, clothes, appliances and all the rest. The MoneySmart site notes a number of very valuable things to do and I fully endorse them. If you are the rare person who consistently puts the effort and commitment into doing all these things, then keep doing so.

Take control of your home finances

If you start with the knowledge that every extra dollar you can put into your home loan is going to save you another dollar in interest, it might just motivate you to get an accurate picture of your spending. I'm not talking about living on a shoestring, but knowing your current spending habits can help you identify the easy areas for improvement.

Often just the action of measuring something sets things on the course of improvement as you are more aware of what is going on and naturally start making changes.

If you are struggling to manage your household expenses, mortgage repayments, and other unexpected bills that always seem to arrive at the wrong time, it might be time for you to sit down and create a budget that works for you.

Most people don't stick to a budget simply because they don't have one.

Having a budget not only helps you spend within your means, it can show you the immediate areas where you can reclaim money and redirect it into your home loan.

Valuable Resource: get your budget planner

The title of this book does have the word "Easy" in it, and I know doing a budget is probably the opposite of everyone's definition of easy. But I think controlling your spending is easier than working extra hours to make up for the wasted money.

To make it a little simpler, you can download a complimentary copy of the MoneySmart Budget Planner from our website – using the link below:

www.mortgageaustralia.com.au/budgetplanner.xls

I won't go into any more detail about cutting your living expenses, but I do think it's easy for most people to find areas where money is being wasted without significantly impacting their lifestyle. Identifying these is a big first step to take advantage of the easier sources of saving you'll uncover.

In short, spend some time on the MoneySmart website; you'll be glad you did.

CHAPTER 16
The magic of compound interest

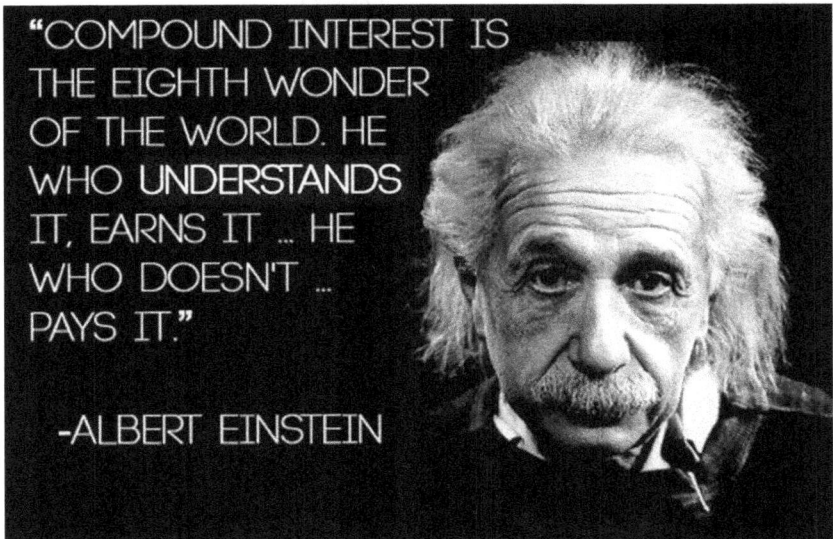

"COMPOUND INTEREST IS THE EIGHTH WONDER OF THE WORLD. HE WHO UNDERSTANDS IT, EARNS IT ... HE WHO DOESN'T ... PAYS IT."

-ALBERT EINSTEIN

Don't worry, this won't turn into a heavy math lesson, but all borrowers must understand the basics of compounding interest to ensure they benefit from it (or at least minimise the damage).

On almost every home loan I have ever seen, including all the major banks and smaller lenders, interest is "calculated daily" and "charged monthly in arrears".

> ### ⊕ Key Point
>
> "Calculated daily" means that if you owe $300,000 at 7%, your daily interest cost is $57.53. So over a 30 day month, it will add up to $1726.03.
>
> "Charged monthly in arrears" means this interest cost is added to your loan once at the end of the payment month.

If your loan settled on the 16th of January, the bank will then add this interest to your loan on the 16th of February and the 16th of every subsequent month. So on the 16th of February you owe $301,726.03. Then, when your $2,000 monthly repayment hit your account, you owed $299,726.

How does knowing this help you?

First - the bad news

If you miss your repayment for any reason, the interest starts compounding—you start paying interest on top of your interest. If on the 16th of February you didn't pay $2,000, you would now be getting charged interest on a debt of $301,726.03.

Actually, it's worse than that. Most lenders will charge a "penalty" interest rate if you are behind in your repayments, usually around an extra 2%. So using the above example, if you missed a repayment you are now accruing interest at $74.40 every day (instead of $57.53). If you miss again it will get worse every month and can quickly spiral out of control.

For that reason, it is very important to get a surplus in your payments as soon as possible. It is also worth considering income protection or credit protection insurance to safeguard against unforeseen circumstances.

This is why you should take the maximum available loan term with a lender that allows you to pay extra. That way you can set your repayments as high as you want, but you can reduce them as well if you lose your job or become ill and could not work.

Now - the good news

Knowing that interest is calculated daily, it makes sense to have money in the loan (or in a 100% Offset Account) as quickly as possible. If you are paid weekly, you should make weekly repayments on your loan.

Also, you should "park" any money that is not currently being used into the home loan (if you have a loan that has a redraw facility). This money will be available as a redraw if you want it later. Every day it is in your loan it reduces the interest you are paying, so your repayments reduce more of the principal of the loan, and in turn you pay less interest next month. This way, you can compound your interest savings.

You should think of your home loan like any bank account, it just has a negative balance so you get charged interest at a high rate instead of earning it a low rate.

It is better to leave your money in your home loan instead of a savings account because you pay tax on the interest you earn, but not on the interest you save.

Make sure you have a home loan that offers a free redraw facility and allows you to make extra repayments at any time at no cost. Some lenders charge a fee to redraw your money, which can discourage you from paying extra.

CHAPTER 17

The most effective repayment strategies

Paying off more in your first year has the biggest impact

It might seem strange, but in the first few years of your home loan, you usually just pay off interest and barely touch the amount that you borrowed in the first place. This means that the interest on your loan won't start to reduce for quite some time if you only make the minimum repayments.

If you can tweak your budget to pay just a little bit more each month, or each fortnight, you might be surprised at what a difference it can make.

> ### Example: paying more than the minimum
>
> On a loan of $400,000, by paying an extra $50 each month, you could save around $36,000 on your total interest – and pay your loan off 1 year and 9 months earlier than expected.

The first year of your loan is the most expensive, by which I mean that it is the year in which you pay the most interest while paying the least off the loan. On a 30-year $300,000 loan at 7%, you would be paying $1,996 monthly repayments. That means that you pay $23,952 in the first year, but you would have only reduced your loan by $3,047.43. You have spent over $20,900 just on interest.

However, the positive to this is that the first year is the time when you can make the biggest impact on the *future* cost of your loan. In the first year, you can pay your loan off twice as fast with a relatively small increase in your repayment. If you increased your repayment by $253 per month for just the first year, at the end of that year, you will have paid off $6,182.71.

You have more than doubled the rate you are paying your loan off, but you didn't need to double your repayments. Not only that, but by having paid that extra $3,036 in the first year ($253 x 12 repayments), you will now save a total of $19,974.80 in interest over the remaining term of your loan. That is a huge amount to save, and it only took a moderate adjustment to the regular payments.

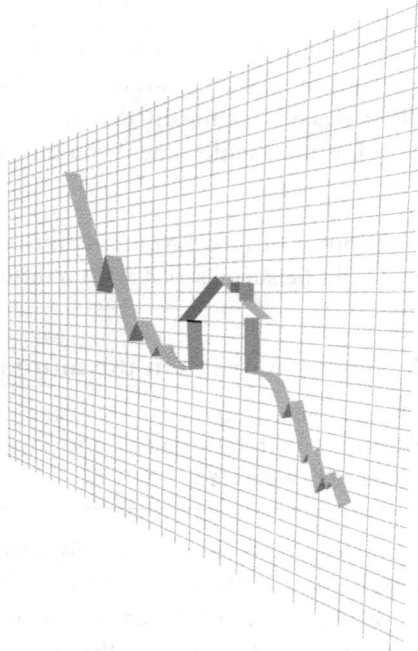

Of course, we all know that increasing your repayments will save you interest, but the key point is that you are much better off doing it at the start of the loan than later on. If you waited until the 10th year of the loan to make these higher repayments, you would only save $9,443.21 in interest.

Do you buy a takeaway coffee every day on the way to work? By saving that $4 per day, and paying the savings off your loan now, you could save about $55k on your total interest, and pay your loan off about 2 years and 8 months early.

Try making a list of all the small things you spend money on daily or weekly, and see if there is anything you could happily do without. Grab a calculator and multiply the item by 52 weeks, and then 25 to 30 years. You might be surprised what you find!

The takeaway here is that extra repayments at the start of your loan are much more effective than extra repayments later on.

That's why I often say that you should view your home loan like a savings account, but with a guaranteed tax-free rate of return that is much higher than any bank's saving account will give you.

Many ways of saving money on your mortgage involve making extra repayments. However, there are also techniques that can save you in interest without having to pay extra. One simple technique is to pay the exact same amount overall, but break it up into smaller, more frequent repayments. It's far from the biggest savings you can see, but it's a simple one to put into practice right away.

The reason this works is that lenders calculate the interest on your loan daily, so, even though your repayments might be made on a monthly basis, your interest is accruing every day—even while you sleep. By changing your repayments to come out weekly or even fortnightly, you will also reduce the total amount that you pay on your loan as well as pay your loan off faster.

Example: the power of weekly repayments

If you were paying $2,000 a month on your home loan, you could break that up into weekly repayments. Instead of 12 lots of $2,000 payments each year, you would make 52 lots of $461.53 each. In both cases, you have made total repayments of $24,000 per year. However by paying weekly, you save $10,510 in interest and shorten the term of the loan by 200 days.

This is not to be confused with splitting your monthly repayment into 4, as there are 4.33 weeks in the average month. If you did that, you would actually pay extra each month – which is course going to save you even more. Some home loans only allow monthly repayments, so always make sure that this feature is available on your loan.

CHAPTER 18

Offset account – how to save thousands without making any extra repayments

About the cheapest way to reduce your mortgage faster is the proper use of a 100% Offset Account, which is like any normal bank account, with one major benefit—any money that is in the Offset Account reduces the interest you pay on your home loan every day.

An Offset Account is a savings account linked with your loan that reduces the interest you pay. Your lender will consider the money in this account and deduct it from what you owe before calculating your interest.

All-in-one or 100% Offset Loans allow you to use your mortgage as your key financial product. This means you have one account into which you can pay all of your income and from which you can draw all your living expenses by using a credit card, EFTPOS, or a chequebook. You also make your mortgage repayments from this account.

Because all your pay goes into your mortgage account, you reduce the principal on which the interest is charged.

These types of accounts can make a huge difference in how fast you pay off your loan. Sure, you might take a couple of steps back when you pay for living expenses, but careful use of this sort of financial product can put you thousands of dollars ahead compared to pay-once-a-month home loan.

Your goal is to make your Offset Account the centrepiece of your finances. You want all your family income to go into it, and you want to keep the money in there as long as possible. Every day that money is in there, you pay less interest on your home loan – meaning your repayments pay off more of the principal so you pay less interest next month, and so on.

Case Study: using an offset account

If you owe $300,000 and you have an average balance of $10,000 in your Offset Account, your lender only charges you interest on the difference, $290,000. At a 7% interest rate, that would save you $700 per year. This can have a significant impact on your loan in the long term.

If you could keep $30,000 in an Offset Account, you would save $153,661 in interest over the life of your loan (and you still have your $30,000).

The alternative would be to have $30,000 sitting in a savings account earning interest. For the sake of comparison, let us say you were earning 5% in a savings account (which is considered income and is taxable). If you were taxed at a rate of just 15%, your

---

Case Study *(cont.)*

$30,000 would now be worth $81,460 at the end of the same period.

So, in most cases, it is much better to keep money in your Offset Account rather than in a savings account. You are more than twice as much better off by keeping the money in your Offset Account.

There is one important caveat—it is rarely beneficial to pay an additional cost for an Offset Account. Most lenders have "Standard" loans that include an Offset Account but are often around 0.5% or more expensive (plus monthly account keeping fees) than their "Basic" home loans that don't have an Offset Account.

> Lenders like to up-sell people into their Standard Loan knowing that many customers don't know how to use their Offset Account properly and will end up paying more interest overall.

An Offset Account can be a very effective strategy for staying a step ahead of your home loan, provided that your spending does not outstrip your savings and particularly if you leave your savings to grow over time. The whole concept fails if you never have any money in there.

The key to making an Offset Account work to your advantage is keeping as much money as you can in the account for as long as you can at any given time. Many borrowers do not take full advantage of it because they don't know how to keep their money in there as long as possible while still living off the income they have pouring into the account.

The trick, as we shall see, is *prudently and systematically* using credit cards.

Offset accounts – maximising the benefit with credit cards

The key to maximising an Offset Account is to maintain as high a savings balance as possible.

The first step as I've said is to have all your income paid directly into your Offset Account. Then, it's a matter of keeping as much of your money in the account for as long as possible.

> **Key Point**
>
> One of the most effective tools for accomplishing this is a credit card with a long interest-free period. Look for a lender offering 55-days interest free.
>
> But don't fall into the trap of overspending or you'll start getting charged very high interest on the credit cards and then you are worse off.

While it may seem strange to use a credit card to save, putting as many living expenses as possible on a 55 day interest free card instead of immediately paying them from your Offset Account is very worthwhile. The interest-free period allows you to hold your money in the Offset Account for as long as possible, maximising your interest savings. You just need to make sure you pay off your credit card debt in full before each interest-free period runs out.

You also need to ensure that you are disciplined with your expenses, payments, and timing. If you are tempted to put too much on the plastic, the credit card tactic can easily become a debt trap.

> If the temptation to overspend concerns you, you may be better off injecting any spare funds straight into your loan repayments instead of turning to an Offset Account.

Look for an Offset Account that still gives you the standard benefits of a regular savings account: ATM and EFTPOS access as well as telephone and internet banking.

Although the aim of an Offset Account is to maximise your savings, you still want to be able to access and use your funds as you would with any regular savings account.

Example: using credit cards to save

If you have an income of $6,000 coming in every month, and you used all of that to pay off your credit cards 55 days later, you would save an additional $61,858 in interest over the life of your loan, and you would never have to pay a single extra cent in repayments.

Lenders often charge a higher home loan rate for an Offset Account. Ask your broker to help you shop around for the most competitive option to suit your circumstances.

If you are still paying off your home or an investment property, but also managing to sock away some savings, an Offset Account could help you be debt-free faster. Talk to your broker about your circumstances to find out which options may work best for you.

Key Point

The important things to keep in mind are:

$ Pay all your income into the single Offset Account.

$ Keep it there as long as possible.

$ Use your credit cards, but pay them off in full before interest is due.

$ Whatever money you can save, save it in your Offset Account.

STEP 7

The millionaires trick to building wealth

In the Introduction I spoke about my own path to mortgage freedom which involved implementing all the steps I have discussed already. These steps allowed me to build equity faster without making significant extra repayments and lifestyle sacrifices. I then used the equity I built to make what I considered to be modest and safe property investments.

This final step may not be for everyone but if you want to really accelerate your own journey to mortgage freedom, this is the fastest, easiest and safest way I know.

CHAPTER 19
My basic plan

Forget about "get-rich-quick"

This is not a 'how I became a property millionaire in 2 years and own 50 homes' story. From watching my own clients over time and continuing to educate myself, I have learned what I believe is a safe, low maintenance and stable process for property investing, and one that has minimal impact on your lifestyle. From my own property investing, I can certainly say that the approach I outline below is what has worked best for me.

Active approaches to property investing, such as renovating or subdividing and building, can be very effective, but they require large amounts of time and effort and things can go wrong if you aren't experienced. Those approaches can be exciting, and TV shows like The Block and House Rules are always popular.

However, in my opinion, investing, when done properly, should be pretty boring. It should involve safe, predictable capital appreciation with time on your side.

I believe the best results are obtained by building an entry-level house and land package in a new land release area in a capital city. Then, repeating this every few years or as you grow sufficient equity and rental income.

You should have at least a 15-year investment horizon, the longer the better.

In my opinion, no investment strategy is as safe and predictable as this. There should be no significant financial sacrifices required and, if followed, provide you the maximum chance of a very healthy (and possibly early) retirement. It keeps your investment in your hands, so you can be as actively or as passively involved as you choose. This approach also provides a good balance between your *cash flow* and *capital growth*.

I will quickly define these two concepts of cash flow and capital growth as they apply to property investing.

Cash flow

This is the difference between how much money it costs you to own the investment and how much money you get from it.

Case Study: negative or positive?

So if you pay $20,000 a year on the investment home loan, rates, and property maintenance and receive $14,800 a year in rent, your cash flow is minus $5,200 each year, meaning that it costs you $100 per week to own this investment.

You are said to be 'negatively geared' in this situation because you can reduce your taxable income by $5,200 when doing your tax and get a tax refund. Whereas, if you were making $100 a week, you would be 'positively geared', and you would pay tax on the extra $5,200 each year.

Capital growth

This is the value by which the investment increases. In a perfect world, your investments make you money while you own them (are positively geared) and are also increasing in value. With property investing, the goal is to minimise your expenses while the rental return increases over time, slowly moving you from being negatively geared to being positively geared, so you can then afford another investment property.

📋 Case Study: working out your return

If you bought an investment property for $400,000 and sold it 10 years later for $600,000, you would have made $200,000 in Capital Growth. In this example, you have spent $52,000 over ten years to own the property ($5,200 per year x 10 years) and made $200,000 when you sold it. So your return has been $148,000.

Land value and building depreciation

The first principle of property investing is that land appreciates while buildings depreciate. That is why I recommend a house and land package, not an apartment or unit.

The land itself isn't deteriorating or becoming less usable; however, the house that sits on the land is deteriorating a little every day and costing money to maintain.

⊕ Key Point

In a 25 year snapshot, capital city house prices had risen 394% and regional prices by 420%. However, land values had risen much more steeply. According to property research group RP Data, from 1990 to 2014, the cost of *land* per square metre increased 710% in capital cities and 742% in regional areas.

The price of land on its own has increased at around double the rate of the price of house and land combined. This is to be expected, because the value of land will always be determined by supply and demand. It will go up and down depending on the demand for the land and how much is available.

If you build a brand new house today, with a construction cost of $200,000, 50 years from now it won't be worth $200,000. In fact, it might be completely worthless and may be ready to be demolished. That is when people refer to land with an old house on it as 'just land value'.

The exception to this is when the price to build increases faster than the rate at which the value of the building itself falls. At which time, you may get the benefit of land and building price appreciation.

> The point of investing in property is to own land, which, as the statistics show, is consistently rising in value.

Perhaps land value doesn't rise every single year, but it historically has risen over any 10-15 year period, and you can be confident that it will rise as long as Australia sees an increasing population. That is one reason why I recommend having at least a 15-year investment outlook.

It is important to maximise the tax effectiveness of your property investment. This is one reason I recommend building your own house and land package, rather than buying an older, established property.

You might be asking yourself: 'Why don't I just buy land?'

It seems logical that you don't want to buy an asset that is falling in value the moment you buy it. Well, the main reason to have a house on the land is that the house gives you an income in the form of rent, which goes towards your costs of owning the land and should pay a lot more than the building cost of the house alone.

However, you still face the falling value of the house. Thankfully, the tax office recognises this, which is a bonus for you known as 'depreciation'.

> Depreciation is an important concept for property investors to understand. It can dramatically improve the cash flow from your property and it can get you positively geared faster.

Depreciation is simply saying that you have an asset that earns you an income but it is losing value.

Don't get too worried about the specifics of this. In practice, all you need to do is to get a Property Depreciation report, which usually costs a few hundred dollars. It will specify the tax deductions allowed for your property, which you (or your accountant) will use when preparing your tax return each year.

Example: depreciation helps your cash flow

To give you an idea of what it means for your cash flow, let's say that on an entry-level 4 bedroom home the total depreciation was $8,000 per year. If you are in the 37% tax bracket, this means you will get an additional tax refund of $2,960 each year.

You can even get that tax refund calculated into your regular pay, so you don't need to wait until the end of the year to receive it. In our example, being out of pocket $100 per week, you are now only out of pocket $43.08 per week.

Depreciation is higher when the property is newer. Older properties do benefit from depreciation, but not as much. After 40 years, the property is considered to have completely depreciated.

New vs old

New properties require less maintenance and generally carry increased tax benefits, but older properties still have their advantages, especially if you are looking to add value through improvements or renovations.

One of the key tax advantages of buying properties built after 1988 is depreciation, which accounts for wear and tear and offsets it against your income tax.

It applies to the external structure and internal fixtures on a property, so even if your rental is pre-1988, you may still be able to claim depreciation for any renovations, including those undertaken prior to purchase.

To claim this tax benefit, you need to have a depreciation schedule prepared by a qualified quantity surveyor. This generally costs anywhere from $300-700, with many companies promising your money back if you are unable to claim back at least the cost of the survey in depreciation in the first year.

The advantages of choosing the right property

There are other advantages to buying a brand new home:

$ You should be able to be more selective with your tenants, as people will prefer to live in a new home more than they would an older, more run down home.

$ You should be able to charge higher rent, as you have a more desirable property.

$ There should be minimal property maintenance costs compared to an older property because new properties usually have certain warranties if items break, such as dishwashers, doors, and air conditioners.

This should also be an entry-level home. A basic 3 to 4 bedroom home is the sort I would suggest.

There are four important reasons for this.

1. You want to get the maximum rent for the price of the house and land. If your house and land costs $600,000, you are unlikely to get $500 a week in rent, but a $400,000 house and land might get $350 a week in rent. There are exceptions to this, but in general, as the house price increases, the rental return does not increase at the same rate.

2. You want the widest possible rental appeal. The higher the rent, the smaller your potential pool of tenants will be. In periods of economic difficulty, the expensive rental properties become harder to find tenants to occupy.

When times like the Global Financial Crisis strike, expensive homes drop in value the most. Median house prices are also affected, but not nearly as much as the top end of town.

3. By buying at a lower price level, you are going a long way towards putting a floor under the price you bought at. If a home similar to yours can't be built for less than yours, you have as much price stability as you could hope for. It always comes back to supply and demand. Demand for expensive homes will always be tied to good economic times, but demand for affordable homes will always be strong, as long as we have a growing population.

4. You are better off owning two investment properties worth $350,000 each than one worth $700,000. You are much less likely to have both cheaper properties untenanted at the same time than you are having the single property untenanted.

Cheaper investment properties allow you to diversify, so you are not reliant on a single property, in a single location, with one tenant. Instead, you can spread your risk in different geographical areas. We all know the risks of putting all your eggs in one basket.

Safety first

One of the biggest concerns of would-be-investors are the risks of them becoming unemployed or having problem tenants who might damage their property or stop paying rent.

The answer is to ensure you are properly insured against these circumstances.

Key Point

Income Protection Insurance and Landlord Insurance are a must when you own an investment property. Don't leave yourself exposed.

I have had one bad experience with tenants where the real estate agent had to organise an eviction and there was some property damage, but our out-of-pocket expenses were very minor and we had the property re-tenanted quickly. All of the hassle of the eviction was handled by the real estate agent.

Where I went wrong was that this was an older property where I was looking to be a bit more adventurous and later knock it down and rebuild. As such I wasn't able to be particularly choosey about tenants — a lesson learned the hard way to keep it simple and stick with the basic plan I've described above. It wasn't a great experience, but the hundreds of thousands of dollars I've made from property means that I am the one laughing all the way to the bank.

👁 Valuable Resource: finding the ideal tenant

Don't make the same mistake I made – instead download my Free Guide To Finding The Ideal Tenant from the following page on my website:

www.mortgageaustralia.com.au/idealtenant

Does it still work?

The question you probably have at this point is: *"Will this work in the future or did he just get lucky with rising property prices?"*

My answer is yes! I'm confident it will work into the future, here's why.

At that time I was paying interest rates as high as 8.25%. So on an interest only loan that is as much as double the cost to hold those properties as it would be at the time I'm writing this. So it cost me twice as much to own the same investment property.

I ended up with a home that was double the median house price of that time. This was relative to my income as my business started to grow, just as the home you end up owning will be relative to your income.

Slow property growth usually results from slower national economic activity, which in turn means lower interest rates. Similarly when property growth is rapid, interest rates are likely to be higher.

Something people are often concerned about is the likelihood of another credit crisis such as occurred in 2008. Personally I owned a lot of property throughout this period and the rapidly falling interest rates, and the fact I owned sensible, entry level homes as investment properties allowed me go through this period unscathed.

I know my properties have all increased more in value since then and I have no intention of selling any, because I consider them valuable investments that guarantee my financial future.

But whether it is been fast or slow, in the long run it has always risen, so I'd prefer to have the wind at my back even if it is only blowing softly for a while.

I'm not saying everyone can or should try and be mortgage free in seven years - or I would have titled this book "Everyone can be Mortgage Free in 7 Years Just Like Me!"

What I will say is that you can definitely implement some or all of the seven steps at your own pace and you will definitely be mortgage free faster than if you don't do any of them.

CHAPTER 20

Making my plan work for you

The next part of this approach is to repeat the process every few years or as frequently as you are comfortable with so you can safely and slowly accumulate a portfolio of properties in different locations and at different times in the property cycle.

As the rental returns increase on your first property, and the equity grows such that you feel you can afford to own another, then you buy another. There is no right rate at which to do this, apart from understanding that you don't want to stretch yourself too thin, but the longer you own each property, the better.

By spreading them out over time you are likely to buy at different times in the property cycle, rather than running the risk of buying multiple properties at the peak of the market. By doing this, you no longer need to worry about trying to time the market.

> I think that people get concerned about the total debt they have, but the way to look at an investment property is by how much it is going to cost you every year to own it.

If it costs you $150 a week to own your current $400,000 investment property, you may decide to wait until that falls to $50 a week, as your rental income rises before you buy the next one. When you buy the next one, you are spending $200 a week on your two investment properties. A few years later, as rents increase on your first two properties you can now buy a third and it may still only cost you $200 per week.

Valuable Resource: property manager guide

Make sure you get a good property manager. It will make your life a lot easier. Download my guide to choosing the right property manager from my website below:

www.mortgageaustralia.com.au/goodpropertymanager

As an example, it may take you ten years to eventually have $1.5M in property with $1.2M in investment loans. If they increase in value by, on average, just 3% a year, that is $45,000 every year that you are growing your wealth, which compounds, tax-free, until you sell them. It is only costing you $10,400 per year (and falling, as rents rise) to own them.

Case Study: quick look at investment numbers

Purchase cost	$420,000
Interest rate	6.00% pa
Weekly repayments	$629
Expenses	
Rates (will vary between councils)	$1,200 pa
Property manager (@10% of rent)	$2,137 pa
Insurance	$500 pa
Maintenance	$600 pa
Total expenses	$4,437 pa or $85.33 pw
Total weekly cost	$714
Income	
Average weekly rent	$4,113

Case Study *(cont.)*

A quick check on the numbers will show $714 per week in mortgage and expenses and an income of $411 per week. This leaves a shortfall of $303 per week. But the story doesn't end here. By using a combination of the depreciation on the property AND your finance expenses against your income, you can get a combined tax reduction in the order of up to approximately $10,000 each year. This reduces your weekly commitment (covering your new investment property) to just $110 per week.

You can even claim your tax refund in advance from each pay cycle to help with cash flow. Search the ATO website for PAYG withholding variation application for more details.

It is now even more important to review your home and investment loans regularly to make sure you have the cheapest possible structure. Run your investment portfolio like a business—keep your costs down and income up. In terms of structuring your loans, the idea is to prioritise your home loan over the investment property loans as your investment loans are tax deductible. You do this by having a principle and interest loan on your home, and an interest only loan on your investment properties. Once your home loan is fully paid off, you can start paying off the investment loans, which is really another way of saving money because you will get it back when you sell them (and pay less interest in the meantime).

To summarise, while no form of investing is guaranteed, my personal view is that gradually building a portfolio of low-cost new homes in new land developments within major capital cities is a safe and simple property investment path.

Valuable Resource: help from an expert

If you would like assistance in where to quickly and easily find and organise the sorts of properties I recommend, just email me at **davidham@mortgageaustralia.com.au.**

CHAPTER 21

Put the plan into action

So now you know what you should be doing.

When setting up your home loans, one of the most important decisions you will make is deciding how to implement these steps, starting with getting the right home loan, setting it up correctly, and reviewing it regularly.

To do this most effectively, you need a trusted advisor.

Find a trusted advisor

The way I see it, the answer comes down to two things:

1. **Trust** – in whose interest is it that you pay your home loan off fast?

2. **Competence** – who knows how to do it properly?

When it comes down to it, I trust people whose own success relies on helping me succeed. It may be a tough way of looking at things, but I don't assume my bank or any other business is going to help me out just because they like me.

People act in their own self-interests, so I want the help of people whose self-interest matches my goals.

After all, you have three choices:

Choice 1 – do it all yourself

Despite all the ads you see about how much your bank or Mortgage Broker cares about you, no one is more invested in you becoming mortgage free than you are.

> Having read this book you should have a good idea of what you need to do and how to compare loans and set things up to best suit you. There is a lot of work and there is a lot to research – but it is an option if you have the desire and spare time.

Choice 2 – go to your current bank or lender

Unfortunately the way the bank makes money is at odds with your goal of becoming mortgage free. The longer you are in your home loan and the higher the interest and fees you pay, the more profitable they are.

I'm not saying your Bank Manager or Mobile Lender is out to get you, but the system doesn't entice them to act in your best interests.

> They can only offer their own loans and if a cheaper loan becomes available with another lender, they simply don't want you to change to it.

Choice 3 – use a professional mortgage broker

A Mortgage Broker is most closely aligned with your goal of becoming mortgage free than your bank is and brokers have expertise across a range of lender's loans.

To be clear, a broker is paid a standard fee by the bank for organising your home loan, so their service comes at no additional cost to you. You might think this must cost you more. However, in reality, the bank is going to pay someone for organising your loan, be it their own staff or an external Mortgage Broker.

Unlike your Bank, a Mortgage Broker has an incentive to ensure you know about new, cheaper loans that are suitable for you from other lenders, because then they are paid the standard fee by the new lender.

Additionally, most Mortgage Brokers don't have anywhere near the advertising budget of even a small lending institution, so they rely heavily on happy customers referring them to their friends and family. There is no greater endorsement than a client who says to their friends *"Our Mortgage Broker helped us become mortgage free years earlier than we would have without them."*

I think, unfortunately, that many Mortgage Brokers tend to be focussed on the immediate task of getting you a good home loan right now rather than the long term goal of your financial independence. They are more about the sprint than the marathon. In my opinion, a 'set and forget' service doesn't cut it anymore.

Key Point

Lenders offer new products and specials regularly, but they don't often pass these onto existing customers.

Be sure to choose a Mortgage Broker whose stated goal is to work with you as a lifetime client and to provide resources and assistance with the ultimate goal of your mortgage freedom.

I'm surprised more Mortgage Brokers don't do this. By helping you become mortgage free sooner, they profit from helping you with borrowing for wealth creation, particularly with investment properties and other assets. It is in the broker's interests for you to get low cost loans and buy investment properties that perform well.

The more successful investment properties you accumulate, the better it is for the Mortgage Broker. It means more loans for them to organise and more happy customers talking about them.

As with any service industry, there are good and not so good providers, but I think any reputable Mortgage Broker that you are comfortable working with, and who focuses on you as a lifetime client, is the best choice.

CHAPTER 22
The Mortgage Australia way

My team at Mortgage Australia specialises in implementing the 7 Easy Steps to Mortgage Freedom for our clients to make it faster and easier for you.

How we help you become mortgage free, easier and faster

$ We charge **no fees** for finding and organising the right, low cost loan for you from over 1,350 finance options with a focus on helping you become mortgage free.

$ We will make sure your loan has the necessary features and is **set up correctly** to be as easy as possible to pay off faster using the smart money management methods I have explained in this book (and avoid costly mortgage mistakes).

$ We will **futureproof your loan** by regularly reviewing it against the latest special offers and better discounts as they become available to you. You can **make an informed decision** about whether to switch, knowing all the costs and benefits of doing so.

$ As you build equity, if you decide you want to invest in property, we can **properly structure your lending** and can provide as much assistance as you require with selecting and organising properties, making it as simple as possible.

> ### 👁 **Valuable Resource: get started today!**
>
> If you would like to start this process, the best way to get started is just to email me directly. Let me know about your current situation and we can work out the best place to start that suits you.
>
> My direct email address is **davidham@mortgageaustralia.com.au**

Some information about Mortgage Australia

$ We hold an Australian Credit License 377294 and are regulated by ASIC.

$ Every local Mortgage Australia Broker undergoes a formal Annual Audit conducted by a third party auditing firm to ensure they are fully compliant with our Licensing and Customer Service requirements.

$ We are 'Hall of Fame' members of the Australian Finance Group. The largest mortgage broking group in Australia which organises 11% of all Australian home loans.

$ We are governed by the National Consumer Credit Protection Act 2009.

$ We are member of the Credit Ombudsman Service Limited. COSL provides a free, impartial dispute resolution service as an alternative to legal proceedings for resolving complaints with a participating financial service provider. If you have any concerns regarding our service to you, here is our Dispute Resolution Process.

$ We are Mortgage and Finance Association of Australia Credit Advisors (Member #9560) and adhere to the MFAA Code of Practice. Our Managing Director is also an MFAA Certified Mentor.

$ To further ensure we are consistently working to meet your needs, we send our clients an optional Customer Satisfaction Survey.

$ There is NO secret or hidden extra cost you are paying. We save the bank's time and money by organising loans for them, so they pay us their standard fee for each loan we organise. A loan organised by us is less expensive for them than having to maintain branches and pay their own full time mobile lender's salaries, bonuses and operating costs.

$ Our loan selection process is completely transparent and objective. You see, updated in real-time, all our best lending options sorted and compared by their real long-term cost to you.

Your next step – take action!

I am never too busy to help another person, just like you, save money and improve their financial future. So I welcome your communication anytime – I'm more than happy to help.

Valuable Resource: start with a no obligation chat

My team of local mortgage brokers and I offer no obligation discussions to help you become mortgage free, faster and easier. Just like I did!

$ You can reach me directly via email:
davidham@mortgageaustralia.com.au

$ For a fast response, complete our online 'financial snapshot' and I can quickly assess you situation:
www.mortgageaustralia.com.au/snapshot

$ You can also get in touch with your local Mortgage Australia Broker via **Freecall 1800 180 800**. Just enter your home postcode at the prompt and you will be connected directly to them.

For plenty more resources, information and to locate your nearest local Mortgage Australia Broker who knows how to apply the strategies revealed in this book, visit us online: **www.mortgageaustralia.com.au**

👁 Valuable Resource *(cont.)*

If you meet with a Mortgage Australia Broker and we can't find a cheaper home loan than you currently have, we will pay you $1,000.00 to compensate you for your valuable time.

Just complete our quick online financial snapshot to get started, knowing you are protected by our legally binding guarantee.

MORTGAGE AUSTRALIA GROUP

$1,000.00
GUARANTEE

$1,000.00 Cheaper Home Loan Risk-Free Guarantee

100%
GUARANTEE

Mortgage Australia
MORTGAGE AUSTRALIA GROUP

Guarantee Reference Code RF458

Go to **www.mortgageaustralia.com.au/guarantee** for more details.

I truly hope you have learnt some new and helpful information in this book.

It's my mission to help as many Australian's as possible achieve mortgage freedom – just like I did – so if you have family, friends or colleagues who might also benefit from reading this book, please pass it on or share it with them. I'd really appreciate it.

A final word.

The most important thing you need to do now is ACT! Unfortunately, information and knowledge is useless if you don't do anything with it – so please take action starting right now, today, and get the expert help, motivation and guidance you need to make your dreams a reality.

Here's to your financial future!

RESOURCES

More helpful information

The following pages contain common questions (with answers) we hear from first home buyers, people looking to refinance or invest in property. These will give you a head-start before you speak with your Mortgage Broker.

The finance industry is full of jargon — so I've also included easy-to-understand definitions and explanations for you. While it's not crucial that you fully understand each of these terms, as your Mortgage Broker should explain everything to you in everyday language, it does pay to be able to talk-the-talk.

Mortgage Australia has helped thousands of people over the last 15 years — so chances are, whatever your situation, our team has seen it before! I wanted to share with you just some of the comments we've received over the years from people all over Australia and from all walks of life. This will hopefully inspire you to take action too!

COMMON QUESTIONS

First home buyer questions

How much money can I borrow?

We're all unique when it comes to our finances and borrowing needs. And different lenders lend very different amounts. Even if your own bank won't lend you the amount you want, do not assume others won't.

How do I choose the loan that's right for me?

Our guides to loan types and features will help you learn about the main options available. There are hundreds of different home loans available.

How much do I need for a deposit?

Usually between 5%—10% of the value of a property, which you pay when signing a Contract of Sale. Speak with us to discuss your options for a deposit. You may be able to borrow against the equity in your existing home or an investment property.

How much will regular repayments be?

Because there so many different loan products, some with lower introductory rates, I recommend going to the Repayment Calculator on our website for an estimate.

How often do I make home loan repayments—weekly, fortnightly or monthly?

Most lenders offer flexible repayment options to suit your pay cycle. Aim for weekly or fortnightly repayments, instead of monthly, as you will make more payments in a year, which will shave dollars and time off your loan.

What fees/costs should I budget for?

There are a number of fees involved when buying a property. To avoid any surprises, the list below sets out all of the usual costs:

$ **Stamp duty**—this is the big one. All other costs are relatively small by comparison. Stamp duty rates vary between state and territory governments and also depend on the value of the property you buy. You may also have to pay stamp duty on the mortgage itself. To find out your total Stamp Duty charge, visit our Stamp Duty Calculator.

$ **Legal/conveyancing fees**—generally around $1,000—$1,500; these fees cover all the legal rigor around your property purchase, including title searches.

$ **Building inspection**—this should be carried out by a qualified expert, such as a structural engineer, before you purchase the property. Your Contract of Sale should be subject to the building inspection, so if there are any structural problems you have the option to withdraw from the purchase without any significant financial penalties. A building inspection and report can cost up to $1,000, depending on the size of the property. Your conveyancer will usually arrange this inspection, and you will usually pay for it as part of their total invoice at settlement (in addition to the conveyancing fees).

$ **Pest inspection**—also to be carried out before purchase to ensure the property is free of problems, such as white ants. Your Contract of Sale should be subject to the pest inspection, so if any unwanted crawlies are found you may have the option to withdraw from the purchase without any significant financial penalties. Allow up to $500 depending on the size of the property. Your real estate agent or conveyancer may arrange this inspection, and you will usually pay for it as part of their total invoice at settlement (in addition to the conveyancing fees).

- $ **Lender costs**—Most lenders charge establishment fees to help cover the costs of their own valuation as well as administration fees. Allow about $600 to $800.

- $ **Moving costs**—don't forget to factor in the cost of a removalist if you plan on using one.

- $ **Mortgage insurance costs**—if you borrow more than 80% of the purchase price of the property, you'll also need to pay Lender Mortgage Insurance. You may also choose to take out Mortgage Protection Insurance. If you buy a strata title, regular strata fees are payable.

- $ **Ongoing costs**—you will need to include council and water rates along with regular loan repayments. It is important to also take out building insurance and contents insurance. Your lender will probably require a minimum sum insured for the building to cover the loan, but make sure you actually take out enough building insurance to cover what it would cost if you had to rebuild. Likewise, make sure you have enough contents coverage should you need to replace everything if the worst happens.

Refinancing questions

Can I get a mortgage where I pay less than I'm paying now?

In almost all cases, yes. But if for some reason I can't find you a cheaper loan, there was certainly no harm in trying. With lenders adjusting their rates outside of the Reserve Bank of Australia, now is a great time to shop around check that you have the right loan for your needs, I am a great starting point. It will depend what interest rate you're currently paying, what type of home loan you have (e.g. fixed, variable, interest only, line of credit) and what features you want in your loan.

Can I consolidate credit card or other debts into a home loan?

This is one of the reasons many people refinance. The advantage is that you pay a much lower interest rate on a mortgage than for most other forms of debt—e.g. credit cards, overdraft facilities, personal loans etc. Providing you have sufficient equity in your property, you may be able to consolidate all your debt on a home loan. If you take this option though it is important to make sure you maintain your repayments at their current level or you could end up paying more over a longer period of time.

What fees/costs are involved in switching mortgages?

Penalty fees could apply if you're paying off a fixed rate mortgage early, but it usually costs only a few hundred dollars in administrative costs to your current lender for a variable mortgage. But I wouldn't recommend a loan where these costs are not substantially offset by repayment savings when you switch home loans.

Property investing questions

What's the difference between an investment loan and an ordinary home loan?

Most of the same types of home loans and loan features apply for investors as for owner occupiers. Some lenders may charge higher rates for investment properties if the associated risks are higher.

Can I use equity in my home as a deposit for an investment property?

Many an investor has started out by utilising the equity of their own home. Banks will usually accept equity in a home (or other property) as additional collateral against which they are prepared to lend. This means you could potentially borrow the full purchase price of the property, as well as all costs (stamp duty and other fees) without having to contribute any cash. The risk in using your home as collateral is that if you can't fund the mortgage for the investment property, the investment property and your home are at risk. When we meet, we can go through the options you have available.

What is negative gearing?

This is when the cost of owning a property is higher than the income it produces. If the rent you get for an investment property is less than the interest repayments, strata fees, maintenance and other costs, your investment is negatively geared, or making a loss. This loss can be offset against your income, reducing your income tax bill.

What is landlord's insurance?

Landlord's insurance provides standard building and contents cover plus cover for theft or malicious damage to the property by tenants and covers loss of rent in certain circumstances. It also covers the owner's liability (e.g. if a tradesperson is injured while working in the property). Landlord's insurance is an affordable extra safeguard and strongly recommended for all investors.

👁 Valuable Resource: do you have a question?

Have you got another unanswered question on your mind?

I'm happy to take questions anytime, just send me an email and I'll help. My direct email is below:

davidham@mortgageaustralia.com.au

JARGON EXPLAINED

Are you thinking about dipping your foot in with property investment, but don't really know where to start? There is a lot of information out there, but many first-time investors become overwhelmed by all the technical stuff. Don't panic though. Here is a list of some of the most common phrases related to property investment—and they have been de-mystified for you.

Capital gain

Capital gain occurs when the property increases in value, over and above what you paid for it, and what you have spent on repayments, improvements and additional costs. If you purchased a property for $200,000, and you spent $40,000 on improvements and $50,000 on repayments—then you sold the property for $350,000, your gross capital gain would be $60,000.

Equity

Equity is the difference between what you owe on your loan, and how much your property is worth. You can build equity by investing in property that is likely to increase in value, while you work to reduce your loan amount. If you purchase a property for $300,000 and you put down a $30,000 deposit you would owe $270,000. Therefore, you have $30,000 equity in the property.

Investment strategy

Your investment strategy is the plan that you make, taking into account your financial goals. Are you looking for a way to get a quick win—and only plan to focus on short-term gain? Or are you looking to build an investment portfolio over a number of years or decades? This could be something to discuss with your accountant or financial planner, as well as your Mortgage Broker.

Interest only loans

Interest only loans allow you to borrow money and only repay the interest for a specific period of time. Usually the interest only period lasts from 1 to 5 years. These loans are helpful if you're focussing on short term gain, and plan to sell the property within the first few years.

Introductory rate loans

'Honeymoon rate' loans offer a lower interest rate for a short period at the beginning of the loan, before you return to standard variable interest rates. These loans can be attractive for owner builders, or those planning to achieve a short-term gain on their investment. The lower repayments mean that you could pay more off your loan balance in the short term.

Line of credit

A line of credit is a pre-approved amount of money that you can borrow when you need it, either as a lump sum or in small portions. This option is popular with experienced investors, who are always on the lookout for their next property purchase, and need to be able to move quickly.

Redraw facility

A redraw facility allows you to make extra repayments against your loan, and then take the money back later if you need it. This is a great feature for people buying and selling multiple investment properties.

All-in-one accounts

All-in-one accounts are designed so that all of your income goes to the one place, and the account is used for your loan as well as all of your expenses. Because everything goes into this account, the amount that you owe will be reduced. Be sure to look into all of the fees involved with this option.

Construction loans

If you're building a home and you don't need to borrow the full amount upfront, a construction loan allows you to only pay interest on the amount that you have spent.

Bridging finance

Bridging finance is designed to help you purchase one property before you sell the other. Once you sell the old property, the funds are paid straight into the loan for the new property. The danger here is if you don't sell the old property as quickly as you thought, you will be responsible for servicing a much larger loan.

Interest only repayments

You only pay the interest on the loan, not the principal, usually for the first one to five years although some lenders offer longer terms. Many lenders give borrowers the option of a further interest-only period. Because you're not paying off the principal, your monthly repayments are lower. These loans are especially popular with investors who pay off the principal when the property is sold, having achieved capital growth.

Extra repayments

If you pay more than the required regular repayment, the extra amount is deducted from the principal. This not only reduces the amount you owe but lowers the amount of interest you repay. Making extra repayments regularly, even small ones, is the best way to pay off your home loan quicker and save on interest charges.

Weekly or fortnightly repayments

Instead of a regular monthly repayment, you pay off your home loan weekly or fortnightly. This can suit people who are paid on a weekly or fortnightly basis, and will save you money because you end up making more payments in a year, cutting the life of the loan.

Redraw facility

This allows you to access any extra repayments you have made. Knowing you have access to funds can provide peace of mind. Be aware lenders may charge a redraw fee and have a minimum redraw amount.

Repayment holiday

You can take a complete break from repayments, or make reduced repayments, for an agreed period of time. This can be useful for travel, maternity leave or a career change.

Offset account

This is a savings account linked to your home loan. Any money paid into the savings account is deducted from the balance of your home loan before interest is calculated. The more money you save, the lower your regular home loan repayments. You can access your savings in the usual way, by EFTPOS and ATMs. This is a great way to reduce your loan interest, as well as eliminate the tax bill on your savings. Lenders provide partial as well as 100% Offset Accounts. Be aware, the account may have higher monthly fees or require a minimum balance.

Direct debit

Your lender automatically draws repayments from a chosen bank account. Apart from ensuring there is enough cash in the account, you don't have to worry about making repayments.

All-in-one home loan

This combines a home loan with a cheque, savings and credit card account. You can have your salary paid into it directly. By keeping cash in the account for as long as possible each month you can reduce the principal and interest charges. Used with discipline, the all-in-one feature offers both flexibility and interest savings. Interest rates charged to these loans can be higher.

Professional package

Home loans over a certain value are offered at a discounted rate, combined with discounted fees on other banking services. These can be attractively priced, but if you don't use the banking services you may be better off with a basic variable loan.

Portable loans

If you sell your current property and buy somewhere else, you can take your home loan with you. This can save time and set-up fees, but you may incur other charges.

Valuable Resource: anything you want to know?

Is there something else you don't understand or would like to know?

I'm happy to assist you anytime, just contact me and I'll help. My direct email is below:

davidham@mortgageaustralia.com.au

CLIENT SUCCESS STORIES

Here are just some of the success stories and comments I, and my dedicated team of local Mortgage Australia brokers, have received from clients over the past 15 years we've been in business.

A saving of $489 a month

Hey Ray, thank you for taking the time to explain it all me. I've taken my time to crunch the numbers, and I always work out how much my loan costs me each week, after I deduct the rent I receive. Currently I must pay a difference of around $239 per week ... with your solution, that comes down to only $126 per week ... that's almost half ... a saving of $489 a month!

Will, Manly Vale, NSW

A daunting experience made simple

A very late, belated "thankyou" for all your assistance to Brendan and me in getting our mortgage organized. For first-home buyers, it's quite a daunting experience, but your assistance made it relatively simple. So a big 'thankyou' from us and we'll be in touch soon as we're contemplating purchasing some more property.

Michell & Brendan Kosmer, South Lake, WA

We saved a lot of money

Obtaining a very good deal for us, where we saved a lot of money. Willingness to fit appointments in with our schedule.

Juliet Vile, Doubleview, WA

We didn't have to do anything

The fact we didn't have to do anything, all the hard work done for us. Excellent knowledge of products and gave us great advice on how the product can work for us allowing cash easily accessible with offset options.

Dara Taylor, Dawesville, WA

I won't be needing another mortgage any time soon

Helping me understand process in another explanation if I did not understand a first time round. Thank you for all your help once again! Hopefully I won't be needing another mortgage any time soon (in a good way!).

Hannah Booth, Sebastopol, VIC

I have already recommended him to my friends and others

Nick made everything easy. A very nice person to deal with and I would have no hesitation whatsoever in referring Nick's services. Nick works for his client. He is sincere, honest, has integrity and a high level of professionalism. Nick has assessed my needs and responded to give me the right product. On the strength of the work that he has done for me with my mortgage, I have already recommended him to my friends and others.

Alice-Maree Bosanquet, Parramatta Park, QLD

Professional – Punctual – Accessible – Knowledgeable – Factual – Detailed

I think the service you provided me was perfect and I can't see any areas that needed improvement. The level of professionalism by Vikki and her team was exemplary. Their knowledge of the product and their leadership to help guide me through my financial matters was extremely helpful. I have no hesitation in recommending their services to my friends and colleagues.

Thor Elliott, Hamilton Hill, WA

Above and beyond the call of your duty

Thank you for all your hard work. You made it easy for us and we appreciate your honesty in dealing with us throughout. I would thoroughly recommend your services to anyone and please send up some business cards, its the least we can do for you. As I've said before, the biggest problem is the banks do it all wrong! Anyway keep up the great work that you do. And by the way, I'd never heard of Mortgage Australia until I searched the Net! Thanks again for everything. I know you've done a great deal for us – above and beyond the call of your duty!!! People like you help to restore my confidence in people. After what we've been thru, it's hard to trust anyone anymore!!! When we are ready to build on, we will be back in touch.

Helen, SA

I was very suspicious of home loan brokers due to the recent bad experience

Dear David,

I was very suspicious of and cautious about home loan brokers due to the recent bad experience.

I am writing to you as head of the Mortgage Australia Group to inform you about the unbelievably high level of service and professionalism provided by one of your

New South Wales agents. In recent weeks my wife and I have had the pleasure of dealing with this agent to arrange the refinancing of our home loan.

The agent in question is Mr Paul Tuddenham who is based in Mittagong and who looks after our area, which is the Wollongong/Illawarra Region of NSW. During February/March I made several on line enquiries about home refinancing through several web sites, including Mortgage Australia. Paul responded to my enquiry via email and gently offered his services.

In making my enquiries I fully disclosed that there were some blemishes on my credit file that were the result of some financial problems that had occurred over 6 years ago and since that time my credit record was clear if not very good. I was also quite specific and fussy up front about what type of home loan features I wanted.

Never have I met someone who has worked so hard and bent over backwards so many times in order to achieve an outcome for a client. Only two brokers responded to my enquiries, one of whom was Paul. Initially, I declined Paul because another broker had responded first and had done some work on our behalf so I felt obligated to this other broker at the time. After some further contact, this other broker advised that no legitimate lender would deal with us because of my credit blemishes. I turned to Paul for a second opinion.

Just to add a little more to the story, a few weeks earlier my wife and I responded to an unsolicited offer of home refinancing from a broker who claimed that we could pay off the balance of our home loan (around $220,000) in less than 8 years. We agreed to an interview with that broker who basically convinced us that it was an offer we could not refuse so we signed up on the spot. As part of the deal the broker charged us around $3,000 for his services as well as signed us up to a lender with an interest rate of 6.90%, which was higher than our existing lender.

In the evening after we signed up I did some research and calculations only to find that we had been deceived in 3 ways:

1. We could not possibly pay off our loan on our current income and commitments within the 8 years as claimed.

2. We had signed up to one of the highest home loan interest rates on the market and,

3. That most brokers did not charge an additional fee because of the commission they received from the lender.

I acted very quickly to terminate the agreement and, in the process, became very suspicious of and cautious about home loan brokers. By the same token, my research revealed that there were products on the market that offered a substantially lower interest rate than our current loan, that we could still dramatically reduce the term of our loan with careful budgeting and that most brokers provided a free service to borrowers. When making my abovementioned enquiries, I also made it quite clear that I was very suspicious of and cautious about home loan brokers due to the recent bad experience. Anyway, back to Paul.

The product was exactly what we had asked for and with a lender who was attractive to us.

Paul responded to my request for a second opinion by stating that he had made some enquiries with lenders and felt that it was possible to get the product that I wanted from a reputable lender and that there was a way of working around my blemished credit history. My wife and I agreed to an interview with Paul.

We had a 2-hour interview at our home on a Saturday afternoon. Paul gently, openly and I believe honestly presented to us a number of home loan options that met my clearly defined preferences. There was no hard sell and, in fact, Paul wanted to leave his information with us to think over first before committing to anything. It was my wife and I who "pushed" Paul to sign us up because the product was exactly what we had asked for and with a lender who was attractive to us because it was a local Building Society with whom we both already had our banking accounts.

After our interview Paul began working on our behalf. He dealt with our lender at a senior level to overcome the obstacles and I know that our home loan application was initially declined but 'saved' due to Paul's intervention and tenacity. It was a long and tedious process, as we were required to overcome several obstacles set by the lender.

My wife and I became discouraged through the process but Paul kept on working hard on our behalf and was continually reassuring that we would win out in the end. Finally, this week, we did win out by getting our home loan approved.

A high level of credibility for the lending industry and especially your company. I have had a lifetime of sales experiences, including a few years of working as a salesperson myself. Never have I met someone who has worked so hard and bent over backwards so many times in order to achieve an outcome for a client. Paul was an absolute pleasure to deal with and my only criticism of Paul is that he works too hard.

I could go on indefinitely about Paul's personal qualities and the quality of his service but my simple point is that Paul worked 'above and beyond the call of duty'. He achieved a high level of credibility for the lending industry and especially your company. I am almost certain that the amount of remuneration that Paul has earned in negotiating our loan is far outweighed by the amount of effort and service that Paul provided. We were a case that most brokers felt was too hard to take on but Paul took on the challenge.

He achieved much more than simply getting a home loan approved.

I know that this has been a long-winded story but I believe that Paul deserves to be recognised and commended at least by your organisation, if not the home lending industry. I am certain that Paul would be embarrassed and reluctant to accept any recognition but he has achieved much more than simply getting a home loan approved.

My wife and I will certainly be recommending your organisation and especially Paul to anyone we know who is entering the home loan market. We also hope to continue our relationship with Paul for future business. I trust that you will find some way of recognising Paul's qualities because he is a role model who has set a standard to be followed by other brokers.

Yours sincerely,

Tad Kiemski, Horsley, NSW

Efficient and expedient

Thank you for the efficient and expedient way in which you carried out the mortgage arrangements. It is just over a month since we moved into our new address and both Jennie and myself would like to thank you for the efficient and expedient way in which you carried out the mortgage arrangements, also the advice which you freely gave regarding the purchase of our new property. We would have no hesitation in recommending you and / or your company, to anyone seeking financial or mortgage advice. Again, many thanks.

Mike & Jennie Tucker, Yangebup, WA

Impressed by your non-pushy, non-biased approach

We are particularly impressed by your non-pushy, non-biased approach to your work. We wish to express our appreciation for the level of help and for the professional manner in which you gave it as a Mortgage Consultant. We are particularly impressed by your non-pushy, non-biased approach to your work; and also for your comprehensive knowledge of the banking sector and real estate industry. Thanks too for the 100% effort you put in at such a busy time of year at the end of December. We're confident as a result to recommend your service to friends, colleagues and family without reservation.

Mark and Mary Muss, Mullumbimby, QLD

Help, advice and reassurance throughout

Thanks very much . . . . ffffiiiiinnnnnaaaaaalllyy, it is going to happen. Thanks for all your help, advice and reassurance throughout this process. I was worried interest rates would be on the way back up again before we got refinanced! This is a great outcome. Talk to you if I have any problems or concerns.

Chris, QLD

Nothing but hugely positive results

My thanks on the congratulations. I may have however had trouble getting past the goal post if it were not for your dedication and professionalism so all my thanks go out to you. You were absolutely correct about locking the rate. I consider myself lucky to have you as my Mortgage Broker and to have listened to your advice. You have no need to worry – after having nothing but hugely positive results with your services you can rest assured I will sing your praises to anyone who will listen. Hopefully in two or three years I will be contacting you again for the purchase of another property if all goes well.

Paul, NT

Knowledge, dedication & professionalism

Just writing to say a very big thank-you for all your help throughout the process of purchasing our house at Kurrajong. Your patience (with my 100,000 questions), knowledge, dedication & professionalism were indeed a great help and made the process of purchasing a property a lot less daunting.

Rebecca Refalo and Darren Briffa

You've been truly amazing…

I've been trying to think of some special way of thanking you for all your help over the last few months and then I receive this email from you with a thank you for us! You've been truly amazing and Drew and I both really appreciate all your support to get us into our beautiful new home. Thank you. We would absolutely LOVE a subscription to Property Investor magazine 96 that would be a real treat! We shall definitely recommend you to all our friends and family who are looking to buy property in the future. In fact I've already given your card out to a friend, his name is Rory 96 so could you please send me a stack? Or drop some into work next time you are passing?

Emma Martin, WA

Clearly understood our needs

Mark provided us with exemplary service — he is personable, empathetic, trustworthy and reliable. He clearly understood our needs and we always believed he was keen to obtain the best possible outcome for us. Practical advice, flexibility and understanding of our needs and family situation. Willingness to meet at our home and out of regular business hours. Just keep doing what you are doing.

Peter Hillman, Mount Waverly, VIC

Love having you as our broker

Just a quick note to say settlement has now gone through finally. Thanks for your assistance and advice all the way through Kat, love having you as our broker and always recommend you whenever the opportunity presents itself. Take care and hopefully be able to catch up when you're down here. Keep in contact, Cheers.

Vikki, VIC
Executive Housekeeper/Hotel Facilities Manager
Hilton Melbourne, South Wharf

Massive amount of effort you have taken to help me

I just want to say thank you so much for all your help and the massive amount of effort you have taken to help me.... I really do appreciate it.

Suzanne, NSW

Prompt action

Prompt Action. Attention to Detail.

Violeta Petreski, Hamersley, WA

We call her "Our Angel"

Vikki was our broker for our settlement for our new house. I believe it is extremely important to give you the following feedback:

Vikki is a WORLD CLASS professional; we could not be happier with her services and her attention to us. We call her "Our Angel", as she always looked after us and our interests. She is extraordinarily focused on her to do's and on her best; that is what make her stand from the crowd.

Only people like her, driven to excellence, will be successful. More than that, Vikki helped us to reach our dream, a new home, and nothing; absolutely nothing in the world is more important than help people to reach their dreams. She adds outrageous value to people's lives... isn't that beautiful? She is leaving a legacy; not only to her children and family, but also to her customers! Wow!

She had a horrible week during our settlement... her father passed away and it was her birthday... she could not even celebrate... she was suffering. Even being all through that, she did not let us down. She just kept it going. I was amazed by her professionalism and strength.

You are very lucky to have a person like her in your team. I am sure you know that... the best only hire the best.

Vikki represents your corporation in a positive and passionate way. I admire her and I am sure she is a natural leader. Being a leader means, in part, serving... sacrifice yourself for the other. Being humble; being simple; being efficient and fast; people oriented. That is what Vikki is.

Thanks for all. Be sure I will recommend your services forever.

Francis, Success, WA

Why go anywhere else?

I would like to say that over the last few years the financial service provided by Katrina Tsiailis to me, through her Mortgage Australia Group has been second to none.

She goes out of her way to explain all the products provided by her, but also the ins and outs of the product she is endorsing. What also amazes me is the fact that she gets the job done without the use of bank jargon. She gives you the choices of all the products she provides.

To put it simply.......why go anywhere else when all your financial needs are catered for ...from refinancing to commercial loans......I am testament to the fact that I have used both services and am more than happy to use them again in the near future.

Constantine Tsigounis, NSW

Would have been so much more confusing without your help

Now that the final payment has gone through, I just wanted to say a HUGE thank you for all of your help, assistance, and endless answers to my potentially silly questions. This process would have been so much more confusing without your help.

It is truly amazing that you are a four hour flight away, and yet my experience with dealing with you has been enjoyable, as opposed to the stressful face to face dealings we had with others along the way. I really appreciate it, and will be sure to forward friends, colleagues, associates, or anyone your way.

Leah Carter, Brighton, VIC

Outstanding communication skills

I would like the take this opportunity to thank you for all your help and efforts — you've been fantastic!! It has been a real pleasure to work with someone who knows their stuff as well as you do — and combines that knowledge with a great customer service ethos, which incorporations outstanding communication skills and regular feedback!! I look forward to working with you again soon.

Nicky, VIC

Found an excellent rate for me

I thought that I had received an excellent home loan interest rate. Whilst "surfing the net" one night I discovered the Mortgage Australia website. I left an enquiry (re refinancing my house) and was rung the next day. I was then put in touch with Mark Lendich and am I glad that that happened.

Mark was able to find an excellent rate for me and and I filled out some papers and Mark did the rest. He was a fantastic help and offered support and advice. I would have no hesitation in recommending Mortgage Australia to all my friends and colleagues.

Anne Hart, South Lake, WA

A real advantage

Sorry for the late reply, been flat out, (usual business, as you know). I would be more than happy to point out the list of services that you've provided me in regards to obtaining my loan and your ongoing help and assistance. I hope my reply to this is not too late and will be of benefit to your business.

List of services offered by Mortgage Australia, that I've experienced:

— Flexibility & Convenient ways of meeting, they come to you.

— Non Biased advice

— Access to an extensive range of lenders

— Outlining their products and services which is best suited to your personal needs.

— This was a real advantage to me and anyone else who's trying to obtain a loan for a mortgage

— They save you the time of personally going and arranging meetings with lenders.

— Friendly down to earth everyday people who will speak to you in plain English to ensure you fully understand all of the terms and conditions set by the lenders.

I was able to obtain a loan thanks to Nigel & Nick Barr, where other lenders turned me away.

I've appreciated the follow up service Nigel has given me even after obtaining the loan, he's assisted me in sorting out minor discrepancies I've had with my lender, and outlined various options available to me If I wanted to re-finance.

Through my experience with Mortgage Australia, I would thoroughly recommend them to anyone chasing the great Australian dream, of owning their own home, and will definitely without doubt or hesitation be utilising their services in the future.

Rick, Berwick, Melbourne, VIC

You delivered a suitable loan before the other two brokers even came back

Construction of our renovation is well underway. I would like to thank you for your professionalism. We phoned three companies who provide mortgage broking services, your response to our initial enquiry was immediate, you visited us at a time that suited us, you listened to our requirements, you responded swiftly and you delivered a suitable loan before the other two brokers even came back. Bill your service was hassle free, customer focussed and it was an absolute pleasure dealing with you and Mortgage Australia.

Ed Geldard, Ferny Creek, VIC

Don helped me navigate this maze

As an extremely busy person, I simply do not have the time to digest and assess the numerous options for home and investment loans from every bank. Don helped me navigate this maze in an easy-to-follow fashion. And Don keeps us informed of new opportunities. I have absolutely no hesitation in recommending his services to anyone contemplating a home or investment loan.

Professor Peter B, Lismore, NSW

Very professional, sincere and a pleasure to deal

Thank you very much for the ongoing assistance you offered in the purchase of our first home. We found you to be very professional, sincere and a pleasure to deal with at all times. We will happily recommend you to our friends.

John Bailey & Katie Scaife, Stirling, WA

Much easier and less concerning on my part

I would like to take this opportunity to thank each and every one of you for the work you did for my recent purchase of property at Ballina. Not only were you able to provide an exceptional service individually, you all excelled by interacting with each other as a team. This made the whole process much easier and less concerning on my part. I sincerely appreciate all your help and once again, THANKS!! I hope to be able to do this with you again someday and will certainly recommend your services to others.

Peter H, Texas, USA

I'm very impressed with the service

Thanks for all your help Claire. I'm very impressed with the service from yourself and Stephen in securing a loan for us. This is a pretty stressful time and you've both made it much easier for us.

Nerida, VIC

Fast, efficient and professional

My Husband & I would like to extend our thanks for the fast, efficient and professional manner in which you acquired for us, a Home Loan with Heritage Building Society.

Margaret & Graeme Jordan, Ormeau Hills, QLD

Good guys like you

Thanks for your email and the sincere advice. Indeed we will persevere with our dream of owning a home in Australia. We will work towards our little goal and would not hesitate to contact good guys like you should we have questions on the way. Thank you so much

Alf

This would have never been possible without your dedication

We can't begin to tell you how much we appreciate all your hard work, time and effort you put into helping us buy our first home. This would have never been possible without your dedication. We will have no doubt in dealing with you in the future and will be recommending you to our family, friends and associates, as I'm positive you will be as helpful and friendly as you were to us. We want to thank you one more time for everything, we will never forget how much you put in to help us buy our home. It was a pleasure dealing through you.

Kym Weatherstone & Garrett Howard, Gold Coast, QLD

You organised everything with a minimum of fuss

You not only source home loans but help people to realise the equity that they have in their home and suggest how they can use this to their advantage.

After making sure you understood my individual needs and my approach to risk, you investigated provider options and made recommendations about a provider that suited both my investment requirements and my every day banking needs.

You organised all the details of the loan with a minimum of fuss. I have no hesitation in recommending your services to any person who appreciates the support and help of a true professional.

Alison C, Alstonville, NSW

We realized one of our major dreams in life

Thanks to Don, we live in an amazing place and realized one of our major dreams in life. We can say we had a lot of luck do be referred to Don — because we got 2 refusals before that and we almost gave it up.

It was a pleasure working with Don — a caring and responsible service and also great results. We would highly recommend Don and his services for anyone that a professional / friendly / ethical and efficient service is important to him.

Danny and Mira T, Eureka, NSW

Suits our particular lifestyle & financial situation

We appreciated your personalised assistance when we recently refinanced our mortgage. You really helped us to find a loan that suits our particular lifestyle & financial situation. We look forward to dealing with you again in the future.

Amber B, Byron Bay NS

I don't think we would have known where to start

Hi Nick, just thought I'd let you know that we are now officially the proud owners of NewWave Systems Pty Ltd. Both David and I really appreciate the assistance we received from you in this matter. Without it, I don't think we would have known where to start.

Serena, VIC

Glided us through the process with painless ease

As newcomers to the minefield of buying land and building Don glided us thru the process with painless ease. The service was impeccable and I have no problems in recommending him to friends needing advice and use of broking services.

Jeremy P, Sydney, NSW

Help from someone who knew what they were doing

I have been meaning to write and thank you for all your help during the loan application process as well as the excellent service we received from your recommended lender throughout. It was so nice to have help from someone who knew what they were doing and could give us good advice about a lender that would suit our needs. On top of that, dealing with the lender in terms of moving all our banking over has been a dream compared with the nightmare we endured with our previous lender when we set up that loan, not to mention the dreadful experiences with their so-called "lending manager" towards the end. When I get some time I will probably write to compliment them on their processes and customer service (and I am flirting with copying it to our previous lender!!!). Anyway, I will certainly recommend you guys to anyone interested in a loan of any kind as our experiences have been so good.

Loretta (and John), Sydney, NSW

Fantastic service in refinancing our home

We would like to thank your company and in particular Mark Lendich for the fantastic service in refinancing our home. We thank sincerely and hope we can do business again.

Kelvin & Julie, Perth, WA

Property is all mine now

Hello Ray.....it's good to read what's going on still..... I discharged my loan a couple of months ago and received my title deed in due course..... a million thanks again for making it all possible!! Please drop in to see my place if you're ever in the area.......

Sandra, NSW

We had fun buying new furniture with the amount set aside in the loan for improvements

Hi Katrina, thanks to you and ING, my son Tony and I have had our first year in our townhouse. We still have a lot of painting to do but we had fun buying some new pieces of furniture with the amount set aside in the loan for improvements. Thank you very much.

Trish, North Rdye, NSW

Smooth handling, even with tight deadlines

Dear Katrina, I am writing to you following our referral to you of our client Mr T & Mrs M of Lake Munmorah. I would like to thank you for handling this finance application so smoothly especially considering the tight deadlines. I thank you for allowing me to attend your client interview at the client's home which you again handled in a highly professional manner. I am told that as a result of your professionalism you will be attending on their daughter & son-in-law's finance application shortly. I note with appreciation that you organised valuation, liaised with their solicitor and kept them constantly informed throughout the process including the conditional approval. You even suggested to clients the option and benefits of the "rate lock". I look forward to working with you again in the future!

Simon Rez, Cartwright & Brown (Accountants), NSW

Cleared the way when I was getting lost

I can't thank you enough for all your help. You were so efficient, and cleared the way when I was getting lost. The house is well under way, although we have had numerous problems with drainage etc, but I am really happy with Joe Hakko and would always recommend him. Meredith, my daughter, will hopefully be house hunting towards the end of the year, and I have given her your card, and she will be in touch. Thankyou, thankyou, thankyou again!

Marianne, Sydney, NSW

Didn't give up until he was happy that he had sourced us the best deal possible

Ray Simpson was by far the most professional, approachable and diligent finance professional we have ever had the privilege to work with. He understood our needs completely and didn't give up until he was happy that he had sourced us the best deal possible for our situation.We can't thank Ray enough for his tireless efforts.

He has helped us achieve our dream that others said wouldn't be possible. Continually kept us updated on progress.Was pro-active to find alternative lenders when we were initially refused a loan.

Extremely approachable and very professional.

Christopher James, Banksia, NSW

Approved and settled earlier then the settlement date

Paul offered us a professional service with attention to detail.We only had 2 weeks before our settlement date to get finance before even getting in contact with Paul. He got my partner & I approved & settled earlier then the settlement date which was a miracle.When we had a question he had the answer, was very knowledgeable. I highly recommend using Paul to arrange your finance as I will continue to do into the future.

We were most impressed by:

— the quick turn around time that you got our finance approved in.

— bent over backwards for us & felt very looked after.

— ran through every little detail of the loan with us to make sure we understood why we did what we did & how it saves us in the long term.

Todd & Samantha Hallas, Currumbin Waters, QLD

Always there to help no matter what time of day

Nick is very helpful, easy to get along with guy and we would recommend him to anyone that is thinking about buy or doing some sort of renovation and needing money. Great advice and always there to help no matter what time of day. Thanks again for your help Nick.

Tyson Palmer, Edmonton, QLD

Always puts my financial gain ahead of his own

I have known Paul for approximately 15 years. He has always delivered superior service for my banking needs and I have no doubt he will continue to do so.

I have recommended Paul to many family and friends as he always puts my financial gain ahead of his own. Always willing to look at big picture...long term and short term. Very approachable.

Brett Lupton, Chermside West, QLD

Informative, professional, competitive, fuss free service

I was most impressed with your attention to detail and follow up. If you would like informative, professional, competitive, fuss free service – call John.

Karlene Smith, Belmont North, NSW

Organises things to perfection

Perfect! Nick is by far is the best the financial advisor I have dealt with, his knowledge and advice is second to none! He organises things to perfection, we hardly had to lift a finger!!

Adam Lamb, Aspendale, VIC

Not fixated on selling one particular product

Mark provides a personalised service seldom seen these days. He is not fixated on selling in one particular product that suits his personal and financial agenda. Rather, he takes the time to get to know what your goals are and the best way of achieving them. I would have no hesitation recommending his services.

Mr. Vaughn Curtis, Belgrave, VIC

Service where the customer always comes first

Vikki's professionalism and friendly service. I was always kept up to date with Helens help also. Between the two fantastic ladies the process was quick and very easy! Vikki and the team provide a helpful and fantastic service where the customer always comes first. She has the right values and I would recommend her services to all my family and friends!

Audrey Greipl, Kemscott, WA

Totally professional and great to deal with

Nick was terrific. From 1 email query to him with a brief on what I wanted to do he was quick to respond understood my needs and how best to incorporate this to get the result I wanted to achieve, I would and have recommended Nick to others as great service reflects his desire to please his customers.

John Davis, Cranbourne, VIC

Nothing was too much trouble

Vicki & Helen are a great team, they provide such friendly professional service, nothing was ever too much trouble & they took the time to explain the whole process & kept me updated along the way.

Helen Norwood, High Wycombe, WA

Wondering why I had not done this earlier

Even though I was hesitant to move from my current lender due to the amount of paperwork involved, he was able to show the amount of savings in interest I would achieve every year as compared to the one off costs of refinancing with a different lender. In the end, I took the plunge to refinance, and now I am wondering why I had not done this earlier. Overall very happy with his service!! Very thorough in looking at all available options and choosing the right package.

Mr. Dinny Devassy Kutty, Shelley, WA

Highly recommend her to anyone

We were able to get an appointment quickly and emails etc were all responded to quickly. We could never ask 'too many' questions, it didn't bother Vicki at all, great service and patience. Vicki was a pleasure to do business with. She was prompt with appointments, returning calls, emails and she kept us up to date throughout the process. I would highly recommend her to anyone wanting help with their finances.

Michael and Linda Fear, Safety Bay, WA

Compared to other brokers, the best by far

Honest, direct communication. Useful education on the brokering business (I understand your role, and how you obtain business from the lenders) Sarcastic sense of humour. Big plus. Wade has been my broker for several years and quickly became a trusted advisor for all my real estate dealings. Compared to other brokers I have used, Wade is the best by far. His attention to detail and ability to communicate have been crucial in closing deals. Furthermore he has always secured the most competitive interest rates for me. Lastly, Wade has a great understanding of the industry, and has provided me invaluable advice through every transaction. I have personally recommended Wade to many of my friends and will continue to do so.

Joseph Ong, Como, WA

A fast result at the lowest price

Don really knows the industry and was easily able to introduce me to the best product for my needs. His professionalism and support provided me with a fast result at the lowest price. Are there any improvements to your services you can make? None that I can think of, you guys are great!

Peter Reynolds, Mullumbimby, NSW

Really took the time to listen to our needs

Mark really took the time to listen to our needs and explain the different loan features. Most impressed with the time taken to participate in thorough discussions regarding the most suitable loan for us. Prompt reply to emails. Attention to detail with form completion.

Anna Taylor, North Perth, WA

Regular contact via email and telephone

Kylie came to our house initially and provided us with lots of information and guided us in our decision. She was friendly and professional at all times. Regular contact via email and telephone kept us informed of a somewhat lengthy process.

Ivan Young, Usher, WA

People don't know who to trust

Comprehensive advice that is tailored to our specific circumstances. I am happy to provide any testimonial that can assist your business at a time when there is so much anxiety surrounding financial advice and financial planning. Your trustworthiness and integrity is second to none in the financial sector and we deeply value all your advice and support.

Sean Maher, Alderley, QLD

Friendliness, professional

Attention to detail, understanding what I was after and why, you came to my office at lunch time which made it easier for both of us, friendliness, professional.

Adrienne Kennedy, Butler, WA

Went above and beyond what was required to help us

Not only was Paul friendly and outgoing from the get go, he was very informative, willing to take the time to answer any question we had and went above and beyond what was required to help us. I will recommend his services to all my friends and family.

Matthew, Gold Coast, QLD

Availability and willingness to answer questions

Availability and willingness to answer questions, no matter how small.

Rachel Bright, VIC

Completely satisfied with your service

Knowledge of lending products available and the processes required. We are completely satisfied with your service. We have recommended you to our friends.

Graham Osmers, Kingscliff, NSW

Ease of applying

Most impressed by the ease of applying and prompt attention to my loan application.

Katrina Haberle, Croydon, VIC

Overall great services

I was most impressed by your availability and easy to contact when we have questions. Passing on information so client get informed all the time. Overall great services.

Pavel Kliment, Hamersley, WA

Drove to Dawesville to make it easier for us

Great advice, very helpful and accommodating even drove down to Dawesville to make it easier for us would definitely recommend to anyone.

Michelle Taylor, Dawesville, WA

Usain Bolt couldn't run faster than the speed at which you helped

Your efficiency across the whole process, from the first phone call to the completion of my finance issue. You made me feel like I was the only customer you were looking after. You kept in contact with me throughout the entire process. Wade, thank you for your advice, knowledge and efficiency in regards to my finance issues. It's been a few months now and I couldn't be happier with the changes. I'd also like to say thank you for assisting my sister with her finances. I don't think Usain Bolt could run faster than the speed at which you helped her with her issues.

Chelsey O'Brien, Ballajura, WA

Great knowledge to get fast results

Great service got exactly what I asked for and very helpful. Organisation and great knowledge to get fast results.

Matthew O'Hagan, The Patch, VIC

Very flexible

I knew very little about mortgages prior to meeting Vikki, and despite asking many ridiculous questions I was never made to feel silly. Very flexible in regards to organising opportunistic face-to-face meetings, ie coming to the airport and Fremantle. Always seemed to remember exactly who I was and details of my scenario.

Jane Livissianos, Derby, WA

Did not seem possible, but Peter made it happen

Peter offered my partner and I service beyond our expectations. Nothing was a problem and everything was taken care of with incredible timing. A settlement in under 4 weeks did not seem possible, but Peter made it happen. We now have a beautiful home we love to live in. It all fell into place. Thank you.

Timothy Bentley, SA

Huge amount of savings

Mark was extremely professional and made everything easy to understand, helping us to realise a huge amount of savings compared to the rate we were on our previous bank. We were most impressed with your extensive knowledge of the industry and how easy it was to communicate with you and we feel that you were doing your best to help us with the transition.

Tania and Bruce Harcourt, WA

Our dream home

Ray helped our family acquire the funds needed to build our dream home at a time when we had started to believe it was never going to happen. Ray was professional and had a wealth of knowledge, Ray was able to do the work behind the scenes that meant we only had to worry about the big stuff and could leave the rest to him. We are now in the middle of seeing our dream home built, Thanks Ray!

Cath Fairs, NSW

MORTGAGE FREE IN 7 YEARS – A TRUE STORY

Below is a true story of the financial journey taken by the Managing Director of Mortgage Australia, David Ham, and how he owned his family home outright after 7 years while only making the minimum repayments each month—and owning multiple investment properties.

The picture over the page is the front page of The West Australian newspaper, showing David and his family when he became mortgage free in late 2007.

David started the Mortgage Australia Group in May 2000 as an individual Mortgage Broker and he and his wife bought their first home, a $104,000 2 bedroom unit in Sixth Avenue, Maylands WA, seven months later on the 28th of December.

In November 2002, borrowing the deposit against the equity that had grown in Sixth Avenue, they bought a block of land for $295,000 in Tourer Court, Maylands with the intention of later building a family home.

In January of 2004 the couple bought a 3 bedroom villa in Babington Crescent, Bayswater WA for $193,000, moving into this property, and again using the equity growth in the Sixth Avenue and the Tourer Court block of land. They kept the Sixth Avenue unit as an investment property and rented out.

Late in 2004, as equity had grown further in the couple's now 3 properties, they started building a home on their Tourer Court land. Their total construction cost for the completely finished home was around $500,000. In November 2005, their twin daughters were born and they moved into their finished home in Tourer Court, which is the home shown in the above picture.

Again, they held onto their Bayswater property and rented it out.

Over the next two years, the couple purchased additional investment properties, using the capital growth across their first 3 properties and growing rental income to increase their borrowing power.

In December 2007, after buying the land 5 years earlier, and in the midst of a property boom in Perth, the couple sold their family home in Tourer Court for $1.62M (the land and construction of which had cost roughly $800,000), and bought a $920,000 home in Bedford with no mortgage needed.

Seven years from when they bought their $104,000 first home, they now fully owned a $920,000 home, and had 8 investment properties with tax deductible interest only mortgages, all generating a rental income and worth more than the mortgages against them.

The basic steps they took were to buy affordable properties that they lived in, but rather than sell when they wanted to upgrade, they held onto these properties. This gave them the maximum capital growth as property prices increased over the seven years, and the maximum equity to borrow against for future purchases.

David gave himself the best chance of success by consistently shifting his debt from Bad Debt to Good Debt.

Of course, a key part of this was rising property prices. There is no guarantee that house prices will continue to rise, all we know is that, historically, that has been the case for Australian metropolitan houses and units over any 10+-year period.

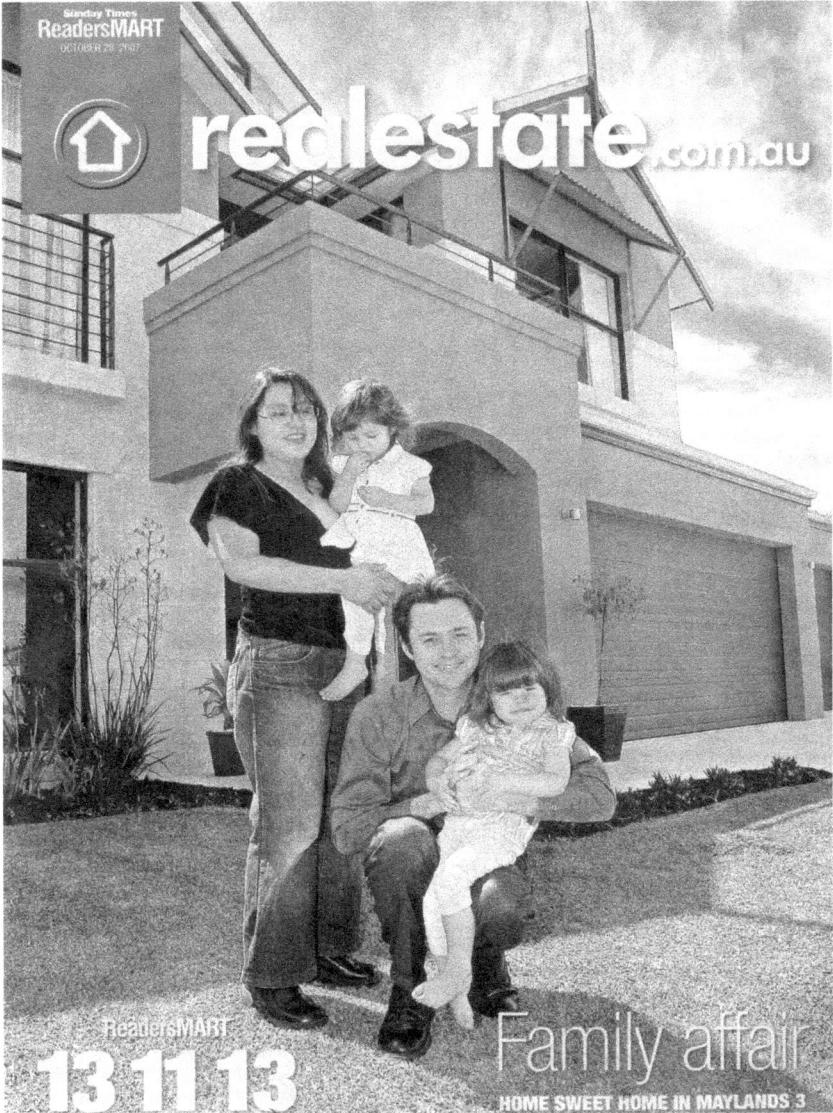

David Ham and his family became mortgage free in just 7 years – using the exact strategies revealed in this book!